DAKHAN HISTORY

DAKHAN HISTORY

MUSALMAN & MARATHA
A. D. 1300-1818

PART I
POONA SA'TA'RA & SHOLA'PUR

PART II
KHANDESH NASIK & AHMED NAGAR

W. W. LOCH

GYAN

Published by

Gyan Publishing House
5, Ansari Road
Daryaganj, New Delhi-110002
Phone: 011-47034999, 9811692060
E-mail: books@gyanbooks.com

Distribution Network
gyanbooks.com
India, USA, Canada, UK, Australia, France

ISBN : 978-81-212-3291-3 (PB)
First Published, 1877

2nd Impression 2020

Printed at: Gyan Press, Delhi.

Dakhan History
Author: W. W. Loch

DAKHAN HISTORY.

MUSALMA'N AND MARA'THA (*A.D. 1300 - 1818*).

Part I.—Poona Sa'ta'ra and Shola'pur.

Part II.—Khándesh Násik and Ahmadnagar.

DAKHAN HISTORY:

MUSALMÁN AND MARÁTHA,

A.D. 1300 - 1818.

Part I.—Poona Sa'ta'ra and Shola'pur.

BY

W. W. LOCH ESQUIRE,

BOMBAY CIVIL SERVICE.

[CONTRIBUTED IN 1877.]

DAKHAN HISTORY.

PART I.

Part I.

POONA SÁTÁRA AND SHOLÁPUR, A.D. 1300-1818.

Introductory.

THE districts which form the subject of this article, the home of the Maráthás and the birth-place of the Marátha dynasty, stretch for about 150 miles along the Sayhádri hills between the seventeenth and nineteenth degrees of latitude, and at one point pass as far as 160 miles inland. All the great Marátha capitals, Poona Sátára and Kolhápur, lie close to the Sayhádris under the shelter of some hill fort; while the Musalmán capitals, Ahmadnagar Bijápur Bedar and Gulbarga, are walled cities in the plain. Of little consequence under the earlier Musalmán rulers of the Dakhan; growing into importance under the kings of Bijápur and Ahmadnagar; rising with the rise of the state, the foundations of which Shiváji laid in the seventeenth century, these districts became in the eighteenth century the seat of an empire reaching from the Panjáb to the confines of Bengal and from Delhi to Mysor.

Early History.

Early in the Christian era Maháráshtra is said to have been ruled by the great Saliváhana, whose capital was at Paithán on the Godávari. At a later period a powerful dynasty of Chálukya Rájputs reigned over a large part of Maháráshtra and the Karnátak, with a capital at Kalyán, 200 miles north-west of Sholápur. The Chálukyas reached their greatest power under Tálapa Deva in the tenth century, and became extinct about the end of the twelfth century, when the Jádhav or Yádav rájás of Devgiri or Daulatábád became supreme. This was the dynasty which was ruling at the time of the Musalmán invasion in A.D. 1294. We find, besides, that there was a rája at Panhála near Kolhápur at the end of the twelfth century, whose power extended as far north as the Níra river. He was conquered by Singhan the Rájput rája of Devgiri, whose camp is shown at Mhasurna near Pusesávli in the Sátára district. The Ghát Mátha or Highland Konkan was from an early period in the hands of the Sirké family.

Musalmán Invasion, A.D. 1294.

The first Musalmán invasion took place in A.D. 1294, but the Yádav dynasty was not extinguished till A.D. 1312. The conquest of the country was long imperfect, and we find Farishtah recording an attack made in A.D. 1340, by Muhammad Túghlak, the emperor of Delhi, on Nágnák, a Koli chief, who held the strong fort of Kondhána now Sinhgad, twelve miles south-west of Poona, which was not reduced until after an eight months' siege.

The Bahamani Dynasty.

The Dakhan remained subject to the emperor of Delhi till A.D. 1345, when the Musalmán nobles revolted from Muhammad Túghlak and established the Bahamani dynasty whose first capital was at Gulburga

Part I.

Poona Sátára and Sholápur, A.D. 1300-1818.

about sixty miles east of Sholápur. The open country acknowledged the power of the Bahamani sovereigns without a struggle. In A.D. 1426 A'hmad Sháh Bahamani changed the capital to Bidar, said by Farishtah to have been an old Hindu capital, about a hundred miles farther east. Farishtah mentions that about A.D. 1436, in the reign of Alá-ud-dín Bahamani, Sholápur was seized by the king's brother Muhammad Khán, who had revolted; but he was soon defeated and the fort retaken.

The Durgádevi Famine, A.D. 1396-1408.

The terrible famine called after Durgádevi, the Destroyer, is said to have lasted throughout Maháráshtra for twelve years from A.D. 1396 to 1408. The country was depopulated; the hills and strong places which had been conquered by the Musalmáns fell again into the hands of Marátha chiefs, and the Bahamani kings had to recover the lost ground.

Musalmán Recovery, A.D. 1420-1451.

In A.D. 1420 an expedition under Malek-ul-Tujár was sent to subdue the Gháts and the Konkan. He put down the Rámoshi robbers in the Khatáo desh and the Mahádev hills; penetrated to Wái and even into the Konkan, and took measures for the cultivation of the land; but the effects of the expedition were not lasting. Another force sent in A.D. 1436 by Alá-ud-dín reduced the rájás of Rairi (Ráygad) and Sonkehr. At last in A.D. 1451 more systematic efforts were made to subdue the country. Malek-ul-Tujár was sent in command of a considerable force. He made Chákan, a village eighteen miles north of Poona, his head-quarters; a stone fort still existing was built there; the hill fort of Shivner, which overlooks the town of Junnar, was taken, and a Musalmán garrison placed in it. Junnar soon became the head-quarters of the Musalmáns in the west, and in a fairer country they could not have settled. Malek-ul-Tujár then overran the lands of the Sirké family, their chief surrendered, and induced the Musalmán leader to march against the rája of Kelna (now Vishálgad). When the invading forces were entangled in the dense wilds he gave information to the rája, who surrounded and massacred the greater number, a fate not unlike that which befell another Musalmán army in the defiles of the Gháts two hundred years later, when Shiváji achieved one of his most notable exploits. A few stragglers retired to Chákan, and quarrels broke out between the Mughals who held the fort and the Dakhan troops; the latter, being the more numerous, besieged the Mughals, forced them to surrender, and then treacherously murdered them, though many of them were Saiads. This story Farishtah relates at great length and with much feeling, dwelling with pleasure on the retribution which overtook the murderers of the descendants of the Prophet.

Máhmud Gáwán, A.D. 1472.

In A.D. 1472 Máhmúd Gáwán, the great minister of the last independent Bahamani king, made another effort to subdue the hill country. He forced his way through the forests, and did not leave the country till he had reduced the lesser forts and finally Kelna (Vishálgad) itself. Subsequently he made a new distribution of the Bahamani dominions. Junnar was made the head-quarters of a province which comprehended Indápur, Wái, the Mán desh, Belgaum, and parts of the Konkan. The other districts on the Bhima were under Bijápur, while Sholápur Gulbarga and Purenda formed a separate province.

Yusúf Ádil Sháh, the founder of the Bijápur dynasty, was made governor of Bijápur; Ahmad Sháh, the founder of the Ahmadnagar dynasty, was sent to Junnar; Gulbarga was entrusted to Dustur Dinár, an Abyssinian; while Purenda Sholápur and eleven districts were held by two brothers, Zein Khán and Khwája Jahán. Ahmad Nizám Sháh went to Junnar about A.D. 1485. He found that Shivner, the fort of Junnar, had fallen into the hands of the Maráthás, and he at once reduced it. He then took Cháwand, Lohogad, Purandhar, Kondhána (Sinhgad), and many forts in the Konkan, and brought his charge into good order.

Partition of the Dakhan, A.D. 1491.

The fall of the Bahamani dynasty was now at hand, and the great nobles had become virtually independent. The first who rose in revolt was Bahádur Geláni, who governed the country south of the Várna river; he was soon defeated and killed. Then Zein-ud-dín, the jáhgirdár of Chákan, rebelled with the aid of Yusúf Ádil Sháh. Next Ahmad Nizám Sháh threw off his allegiance in 1489: he was attacked by Zeinud-dín, but the latter was driven into the fort of Chákan; the fort was stormed and Zein-ud-dín killed in the fight. About this time (A.D. 1489) Yusúf Ádil Sháh of Bijápur also asserted his independence and made himself master of the country as far north as the Bhima.

The new kings of the Dakhan made a kind of partition treaty in A.D. 1491, by which the country north of the Níra and east of Karmála, together with some of the present Sholápur districts, were assigned to the Nizám Sháh king, while the country south of the Níra and Bhima was allotted to the Bijápur sovereign. The lesser chiefs who had joined in the revolt against the Bahamani kings were gradually subdued by the more powerful. Dastur Dinár, who held Gulbarga, was defeated and driven away in A.D. 1495, and again in A.D. 1498 by Yusúf Ádil Sháh; but he returned each time, and it was not till A.D. 1504 that he was finally defeated and killed and Gulbarga annexed to the Bijápur dominions.

The districts of Purenda and Sholápur were held as mentioned above by the brothers Khwája Jahán and Zein Khán. In a quarrel between them, Ahmad Nizám Sháh took the part of Khwája Jahán and Yusúf Ádil Sháh that of Zein Khán, who was thus enabled to get possession of the five and a half districts round Sholápur. These he held till after the death of Yusúf Ádil Sháh. Kamál Khán, the regent, who ruled during the minority of Yusúf's son, wished to supplant the young king, and arranged with Amir Berid, the minister of the Bahamani king at Bidar, that he should be allowed to take Sholápur, while Amir Berid took the districts lately held by Dastur Dinár, and that both of them should dethrone their masters. In accordance with this agreement he besieged and took Sholápur in 1511, which with its districts was annexed to Bijápur. Amir Berid took Gulbarga, but Kamál Khán was soon after assassinated, and Gulbarga recovered. Purenda and its five and a half districts remained for many years under Khwája Jahán, who seems to have been a half-independent vassal of the king of Ahmadnagar.

Part I.

POONA SÁTÁRA AND SHOLÁPUR, A.D. 1300-1818.

Ahmadnagar and Bijápur, A.D. 1524-1550.

In A.D. 1523, when, after one of their numerous wars, peace was made between the kings of Bijápur and Ahmadnagar, the sister of Ismael Ádil Sháh was given to Burhán Nizám Sháh and Sholápur was promised as her dowry, but it was not given up. During the next forty years the claim to Sholápur by the Nizám Sháh kings was the cause of constant wars. In A.D. 1524, in A.D. 1528, and in A.D. 1531, Burhán Nizám Sháh invaded the Sholápur districts, and each time he was defeated. Again in A.D. 1542 he overran them and made them over to Khwája Jahán, but they were restored on peace being made in the following year. Once more in 1548, Burhán took Gulbarga and Kalyán, and inflicted a severe defeat on Ibráhím Ádil Sháh; and the next year he took Sholápur, again defeating the Bijápur forces; and for some years he held the conquered districts. Irritated at his defeats Ibráhím Ádil Sháh suspected the fidelity of one of his chief nobles Seif Ein-ul-Mulk Geláni, and drove him into revolt by his harsh treatment; he retired into the Mán desh, and by degrees overran the country as far south as Miraj, defeating the detachments sent against him, and finally an army commanded by the king in person, whom he drove into Bijápur. In this difficulty Ibráhím applied to Rámráj, king of Bijánagar, who sent a force which defeated Seif Ein-ul-Mulk and forced him to fly to the Ahmadnagar territory, where he was killed.

After his accession to the throne, Áli Ádil Sháh, son of Ibráhím, made an alliance with Rámráj and attacked the king of Ahmadnagar. In the war which followed, the latter was borne down by the superior forces of his enemies and his capital was twice besieged, but he still held the fort of Sholápur. At last (A.D. 1563) the Musalmán kings, alarmed at the power of Rámráj, and disgusted with his insolence, formed a league against him. Husain Nizám Sháh gave his sister Chánd Bibi to Áli Ádil Sháh and with her Sholápur and its districts,

Battle of Tálikot, A.D. 1564.

and next year was fought the great battle of Tálikot, which resulted in the death of Rámráj and the complete defeat of his army.

For some years there was peace; but in A.D. 1590 Diláwar Khán, who had been regent of Bijápur, fled to Ahmadnagar, and urged Burhán Nizám Sháh II. to try and recover Sholápur. In A.D. 1592 they advanced into the Bijápur territory, but Ibráhím Ádil Sháh managed to win back Diláwar Khán; and having got him into his power, sent him as a prisoner to the fort of Sátára and quickly forced the Ahmadnagar troops to retire.

The Mughals, A.D. 1600.

Soon after this the Mughal princes of Delhi began to invade the Dakhan, and in A.D. 1600 Ahmadnagar fell. The country was however only temporarily subdued, and was speedily recovered by Malek Ambar, an Abyssinian chief, who made Aurangábád, then called Kharki, the capital of the Nizám Sháh kings. In A.D. 1616, Sháh Jahán again conquered the greater part of the Ahmadnagar territory; but in A.D. 1629 the country was given up by the Mughal governor Khán Jahán Lodi. A war ensued, and in A.D. 1633 Daulatábád was taken and the king made prisoner; but Shahji Bhonsla, one of the leading Marátha chiefs, set up another member of the royal family, overran the Gangthari and Poona districts, and with the help of the Bijápur troops drove back the Mughals from Purenda. Sháh Jahán now marched into the Dakhan in person, besieged Bijápur, and forced the king to come to terms (A.D. 1636). The country seized by Sháhji was then easily recovered; that chief surrendered in A.D. 1637, and the Nizám Sháh dynasty came to an end. The country north of the Bhima, including Junnar, was annexed to the Mughal territory, and that south of it was made over to Bijápur. Sháhji took service under the king of Bijápur, and received the jáhgir of Poona and Supa, to which Indápur Bárámati and the Máwal country near Poona were added.

The Maráthás.

Under the Bijápur kings the Maráthás began to make themselves conspicuous. The Bárgis or light horse furnished by the Marátha chiefs played a prominent part in the wars with the Mughals; the less important forts were left in their hands, and the revenue was collected by Hindu officers under the Musalmán Mokásdárs. Several of the old Marátha families received their offices of deshmukh and sardeshmukh from the Bijápur kings. The kingdom of Bijápur was destined to survive that of Ahmadnagar by fifty years; but, weakened by its powerful Mughal neighbour and by internal dissensions, it was gradually falling to pieces. This was the opportunity for the predatory Marátha chiefs, and a leader arose in Shiváji, the son of Sháhji Bhonsla, who knew how to unite the Maráthás into a nation by inspiring them with a hatred for their Musalmán masters, and how to take advantage of the constant quarrels and increasing weakness of those masters.

Shiváji Bhonsla, A.D. 1627-1680.

The ancestors of Shiváji come from Verola or Ellora. Máloji, Shiváji's grandfather, was the first of the family who rose to note. He married the sister of the náik of Phaltan, and about the beginning of the seventeenth century was put in charge of Shivner and Chákan and received the districts of Poona and Supa in jáhgir. His son Sháhji married the daughter of Lokhji Jádhav of Sindkhed, one of the chief nobles of the Nizám Sháh court, and Shiváji was born at Shivner in A.D. 1627. The jáhgir obtained by Sháhji from the king of Bijápur was managed by a Bráhman named Dádáji Kondev, who had also charge of Shiváji. Dádáji made Poona his head-quarters, and his management of the districts was able and successful. Sháhji was for many years employed in the Karnátak, where another large jáhgir had been granted to him.

When Shiváji grew up he associated much with the Máwalis, the men of the wild country west of Poona, and began to think of establishing himself as an independent chief. To this end, in A.D. 1646 he obtained from the commandant the surrender of the fort of Torna in the rugged country near the sources of the Níra river. While he sent agents to Bijápur to make excuses for his conduct, he began to build another fort on a hill called Morbadh, to which he gave the name of Ráygad (A.D. 1647). Dádáji Kondev died about this time, and Shiváji took charge of the jáhgir, appropriating the revenues to his own use. He then set to work to gain the forts not already in his possession. Chákan was in charge of Phirangoji Narsála, whom he won over and left in command. He obtained Kondána by bribing the Musalmán commandant; he surprised Supa, which was held by Báji Mohita, the brother of his father's second wife; and finally he interfered in the

Part I.

Poona Sátára and Sholápur, A.D. 1300-1818.

Shiváji's Exploits, A.D. 1648-1658.

quarrels of the sons of the commandant of Purandhar, and secured the fort. Having thus gained a firm hold of his father's jáhgir, he began to make encroachments on the adjoining country. The district south of the Níra, from the Gháts as far east as Shirwal, was in charge of Bándal, the deshmukh of the Hardas Máwal. His head-quarters were at Rohira. There was a Musalmán Mokásdár at Wái who held the fort of Pándugad, and the hills from the Krishna to the Várna were under the rája of Jávli, a member of the Moré family, which had dispossessed the Sirkés, the old rulers of the Gháts. A Musalmán governor was stationed at Kalyán in the Konkan.

In A.D. 1648 Shiváji surprised Lohogad, the state prison of the Ahmadnagar kings, and Rájmáchi, both in the Máwals, and several forts in the Konkan including Rairi or Ráygad; meanwhile Ábáji Sondev, one of his Bráhman adherents, pushed on to Kalyán near Bombay, took the town, and made the governor prisoner. Shiváji at once took possession of the district appointing Ábáji subhedár. The Bijápur court could not overlook this open rebellion, and orders were given to Báji Ghorpade of Mudhol to arrest Sháhji, who was suspected of encouraging Shiváji. Báji accomplished his task by treachery, for which he afterwards paid dearly, and Sháhji was kept in confinement till A.D. 1653, during which time Shiváji was obliged to remain quiet. On his father's release he again began to plan attacks on the neighbouring country. The rája of Jávli had resisted all his endeavours to win him over, and Shiváji therefore sent his agents Rágho Ballál and Sambháji Káwaji to examine the country. They suggested that the rája might easily be assassinated, and Shiváji approved of their idea. He collected a strong force in the forests round Mahábaleshvar, and when his agents had murdered the rája and his brother, the troops attacked and stormed Jávli and soon reduced the fort of Vásota and the surrounding country (A.D. 1653). Shiváji next turned on the deshmukh of the Hardas Máwal, stormed the fort of Rohira, and killed him in the fight. To strengthen his hold of the country, he directed a fort to be built at the source of the Koyna river near Mahábaleshvar; the work was carried out by Moro Pant Pingle, and the fort was called Pratápgad.

Shiváji now ventured to attack the territory of the Mughals, and in May 1657 he surprised the town of Junnar and carried off much plunder to Ráygad. The disturbances which took place in Hindustán through the rivalry of the sons of Sháh Jahán prevented his inroads from being punished. At last, in A.D. 1659 the Bijápur government determined to make an effort to suppress him, and sent a strong force under Afzul Khán against him. Afzul Khán proceeded as far as Wái, and then sent a Bráhman named Gopináth Pant to treat with Shiváji, who had made professions of submission. Shiváji won over the Bráhman, who in his turn persuaded Afzul Khán to have a personal interview with Shiváji, who was then at Pratápgad. The Musalmán army marched to Jávli, while Shiváji brought all his forces under Moro Pant Pingle and Netáji Pálkar and surrounded them. He then, attended by Tánáji Málusra, one of his oldest friends, met Afzul Khán who was accompanied by a single armed follower, stabbed him, and

Part I.

Poona Sátára and Sholápur, A.D. 1300-1818.

Shiváji's Murderous Attack on Afzul Khán, A.D. 1659.

gave the signal for the assault to his troops. The Musalmán army, bewildered at the loss of its chief, gave way, and was utterly dispersed. Shiváji followed up his success with vigour. Panhála and Páwangad surrendered to Annáji Dattu, one of his officers, while he himself took Vasantgad, Rangna, Kelna (Vishálgad), and all the neighbouring forts. A force was sent against him, but he routed it and plundered the country as far as Bijápur. Next year (A.D. 1660) another army was sent against him under Sidi Johár, when he retired to Panhála, where he was closely besieged for some months, and at last, despairing of holding out, he escaped by stratagem to Rangna. The Mughals, disheartened by their want of success, made no further progress until early in A.D. 1661, when Áli Ádil Sháh marched in person to Karad, and thence to Panhála, which he reduced. Many other forts were surrendered to him, but he was called off by a rebellion in the Karnátak, and directed Báji Ghorpade and a Musalmán noble to prosecute the war. Shiváji took this opportunity of revenging himself on Báji Ghorpade for his father's capture, surprised and killed him at Mudhol, and the expedition was stopped. It was soon after this (A.D. 1662) that Shiváji changed his head-quarters from Rájgad to Ráiri, which he called Ráygad. He had public offices built there by Ábáji Sondev, and Ráygad remained the capital of the Maráthás for nearly forty years.

Attacks Sháista Khán, A.D. 1664;

As Shiváji's incursions into the Mughal territory continued, Aurangzíb sent a force against him under Sháista Khán, who made Poona his head-quarters. He then besieged Chákan, but though a small fort, it held out under Phirangoji Narsala for nearly two months; and Sháista Khán, discouraged by the difficulty of his first undertaking, did little else. While he was at Poona Shiváji performed one of his best known feats. He descended with a few followers from Sinhgad, entered Poona unperceived, and surprised Sháista Khán, who was living in Shiváji's old house. Sháista Khán escaped with a wound, but most of his attendants and his son were killed. Shiváji then retired to Sinhgad in safety, and next day a body of Mughal horse, which rode out towards Sinhgad, was surprised and routed by Netáji Pálkar. The Mughals soon afterwards withdrew leaving strong garrisons in Chákan and Junnar. Shiváji now extended his ravages from Surat in one direction to Bárcelor in the other, till at last Aurangzíb was roused, and in A.D. 1665 sent a large army under Rája Jáysing and Dilir Khán against him. They occupied Poona, and while Dilir Khán besieged Purandhar, Jaysing blockaded Sinhgad and pushed on to Ráygad. Purandhar made a gallant defence; but Shiváji feeling he was unable to resist longer, came into Jaysing's camp, and agreed to surrender all his forts but twelve, and to join the Mughal army in the war against Bijápur. His offer was accepted, and he accordingly accompanied the Mughal army on its march, and on the way the Phaltan district was overrun and the fort of Tátora stormed by Shiváji's troops. While the war was going on, Shiváji, in A.D. 1666, having given over charge of the territory that remained in his possession to Moro Pant Pingle, Ábáji Sondev, and Annáji Dattu, went to Delhi to pay his respects to Aurangzíb; but being slighted, and treated as a prisoner, he escaped and returned to the Dakhan at the end of the year. The Mughal

And Surrenders to Jaysing.

Shiváji's Visit to Delhi, A.D. 1666.

Part I.

Poona Sátara and Sholápur, A.D. 1300-1818.

army, which had failed to take Bijápur, had in the meantime retired, leaving garrisons in Lohagad, Sinhgad, and Purandhar; the other forts were either dismantled or left in charge of a weak party, and they were all reoccupied by Moro Pant.

Shiváji Active Again, A.D. 1677.

Soon after his return from Delhi in 1667, Shiváji opened communications with Sultán Mázum, son of Aurangzíb, then governor of the Dakhan, which ended in Shiváji being confirmed in his jáhgir of Poona, Súpa, and Chákan, the fortresses of Purandhar and Sinhgad being retained by the Mughals. It was not till A.D. 1670 that Shiváji made any attempt to recover them. Aurangzíb had directed the capture of Pratáp Ráo Gujar and the body of horse which were with Sultán Mázum; they escaped, and in retaliation Shiváji planned the capture of these important forts. Sinhgad was stormed after a desperate fight by a body of Máwalis headed by Tánáji Málusra, who fell in the action, and Purandhar was taken soon after with less difficulty. An attempt on Shivner failed, but Lohogad was surprised and several forts to the north of Junnar were captured by Moro Pant.

Aurangzíb's Second Effort to crush Shiváji, A.D. 1671.

In 1671 another effort was made by Aurangzíb, and a force despatched under Mohábat Khán against Shiváji. One half attacked Chákan and the other half the fort of Sálher. Chákan was taken by the next year; but the detachment at Salher was utterly defeated by the Maráthás under Moro Pant and Pratáp Ráo Gujar, and the Mughals hastily retreated to Aurangabád.

Soon after this (A.D. 1671) Áli Ádil Sháh died at Bijápur, and Shiváji took advantage of the confusion which ensued to recover Panhála and sack Hubli. In May 1672 he surprised Párli and then attacked the neighbouring fort of Sátára, the state prison of Bijápur, which held out till September The forts of Chandan, Wandan, Pandugad, Nándgiri, and Tátora all fell into his hands in the same campaign. The Bijápur troops made two attempts to recover Panhála, but without success, though in one action Pratáp Ráo Gujar was killed, and his army would have been routed but for the exertions of Hasáji Mohita and two of his officers, afterwards well known as Santaji Ghorpade and Dhanáji Jádhav. Shiváji gave Hasáji the title of Hambir Ráo and the office of Sarnobat, which had been held by Pratáp Ráo Gujar.

Shiváji Crowned, A.D. 1674.

In June 1674 Shiváji ventured openly to declare his independence by being formally crowned at Ráygad; his ministry was reformed, and new names were given to the offices. His chief ministers (Asht Pradhán) were Moro Pant Pingle Peshwa or Mukhya Pradhán, Rámchandra Pant Bawrikar the son of Ábáji Sondev Mujumdár or Pant Amát, Annáji Dattu Pant Sachiv, Hambir Ráo Mohita Senápati, and Janárdan Pant the Sámant. Of the officers not among the Asht Pradhán the chief was Báláji Auji, his chitnis, a Parbhu. In 1675 Shiváji again began hostilities with the Mughals, and Moro Pant retook several of the forts near Junnar, but again failed in an attempt on Shivner. Shiváji also regained the forts between Panhála and Tátora; but while he was occupied in the Konkan with the siege of Phonda, these forts were taken by the deshmukhs of Phaltan and Maláwdi acting for the king of Bijápur. Next year Shiváji again recovered them; and, in order

Shiváji's Expedition to the Karnátak, A.D. 1678.

to strengthen his hold on the country, he built the intermediate forts of Vardangad, Bhushangad, Sadáshivgad, and Machandragad. Having completed these arrangements he set out on an expedition to the Karnátak, where he took Jinji, Bellári, and other forts, and overran his father's jáhgir round Bangalor held by his half brother Venkáji. He returned to Ráygad about the middle of A.D. 1678, and next year made an alliance with Bijápur, which was threatened by the Mughal army under Dilir Khán. Unable to divert the Mughals from the siege of Bijápur, Shiváji ravaged the country north of the Bhíma, penetrating as far as Jálna about thirty miles south of Ajánta; but on his return he was intercepted by a force near Sangamner, and made his way to the hill fort of Patta only after a hard-fought action. Here he stayed till he was recalled south by the entreaties of the regent of Bijápur and the desertion of his son Sambháji to the Mughals. His troops cut off the supplies of the Mughal army, defeated two detachments, and forced Dilir Khán to raise the siege, while Sambháji returned to his father. Soon after this Shiváji died at Ráygad in April 1680. At the time of his death he held the country from the Harankáshi river on the south to the Indráyani river on the north. Supa Indápur and Bárámati were his jáhgir districts, and the forts between Tátora and Panhála mark his boundary on the east. Besides this tract he had territories in the Konkan, in the Karnátak, in Baglán, and in Khándesh.

His Death, A.D. 1680.

Sambháji.

Shiváji left two sons, Sambháji and Rám Rája, the former of whom was in confinement at Panhalla. The majority of the ministers desired to put Rám Rája on the throne; and Sambháji, who managed to get possession of Panhála, was besieged there by Janárdan Pant Sumant. He contrived, however, to win over a body of the besieging troops, surprised Janárdan Pant in Kolhápur, and being joined by Hambir Ráo Mohita and others of the ministers, he marched to Ráygad, which surrendered. He now revenged himself savagely on his opponents, putting to death Rám Rája's mother Soyrábái Sirké and several officers, and throughout his reign his cruelty and violence made him an object of dislike to his countrymen. Nor did intrigues against him cease. In A.D. 1681 a plot was formed by members of the Sirké family, to which Rám Rája's mother had belonged. In this Annáji Dattu, the Pant Sachiv, and Báláji Auji Chitnis being implicated, both of these old servants of Shiváji were executed.

Aurangzib, A.D. 1684.

The usual inroads took place into the Mughal territory, and at last Aurangzib determined to take command of his army in person, and arrived at Ahmadnagar in the year A.D. 1684. He sent out detachments to reduce the forts in the Gangthari, and, in A.D. 1685, while his son Ázam Sháh took Sholápur and so began the war with Bijápur, Khán Jahán took Poona and the open country north of Sinhgad. The emperor then marched to Sholápur, and thence to Bijápur, which fell in October 1686, and the country round at once submitted to him. Eleven months later Golkonda surrendered, and Aurangzib was left in apparent possession of the whole country, which he endeavoured to bring into better order.

Part I.

Poona Sátára and Sholápur, A.D. 1300-1818.

Shirzi Khán, a Bijápur noble who had joined the emperor, invaded the Sátára districts, but was met and defeated at Wái by Hambir Ráo the Senápati, who himself fell in the action, and for a time the Maráthás recovered much of the open country: but Sambháji was daily growing more imbecile and indolent under the influence of his favourite a Kanoja Bráhman named Kalusha. No organized resistance could be made, and in A.D. 1689 the country was again subdued by the Mughals as far as the hills, and the forts between Tátora and Panhála were taken.

Sambháji's Execution, A.D. 1689.

Aurangzíb now marched to Akluj on the Níra, and then to Tulápur at the junction of the Indráyani with the Bhíma, intending to subdue the hill country thoroughly; and while there Sambháji was brought in as a prisoner and executed (August 1689). He had been captured by a Mughal officer named Takarib Khán and his son Ikhlas Khán in command at Kolhápur, who had penetrated to Sangmeshvar in the Konkan, and surprised him with his favourite Kalusha.

Rám Rájá.

Sambháji left a child named Shiváji afterwards known as Sháhu; but as he was only six years old, Sambháji's brother Rám Rája was made regent. The Marátha chiefs now met to decide on a plan for opposing Aurangzíb, whose power may well have seemed to them overwhelming. They decided that the principal forts should be carefully garrisoned; that Rám Rája should move from one fort to the other, and if hard pressed should retire to Jinji in the Karnátak. The Marátha chiefs were to plunder and annoy the enemy in their old fashion. The principal men at this time were Pralhád Niráji son of the late Nyáyádhish Pradhán, Janárdan Pant Sámant, Rámchandra Pant Bourikar Amát, Máhádáji Náik Pánsambal the Senápati, Santáji Ghorpade, Dhanáji Jádhav, and Khanderáo Dábháde.

Sháhu a Prisoner, A.D. 1690.

The Mughals continued to advance, and in A.D. 1690 Ráygad fell and Sháhu was made prisoner. On this Rám Rája made his escape to Jinji, accompanied by Pralhád Niráji, Santaji Ghorpade, Dhanáji Jádhav, and Khanderáo Dábháde, while Rámchandra Pant was left in charge of the hill districts with a Bráhman named Parashrám Trimbak under him. His head-quarters were at Sátára. Santáji Ghorpade was soon after made commander-in-chief, and was sent with Dhanáji Jádhav to collect men and plunder the Mughals, while Pralhád Niráji, who stayed at Jinji, was made Pratinidhi. Against them and the other Marátha chiefs Aurangzíb made little progress. Rámchandra Pant kept his own districts clear, and even surprised the Mughal fauzdár of Wái. It was under Rámchandra's command that the heads of the families of Pavár, Thorát, and Atáwla came under notice. Aurangzíb, in A.D. 1694, after moving slowly along the banks of the Bhíma, at last fixed on Brahmapuri, a village on that river, as his head-quarters, and built a cantonment, where he stayed five years.

Meanwhile the siege of Jinji had been going on in a desultory manner. Santáji and Dhanáji inflicted several defeats on Mughal detachments, and once forced them to raise the siege; but at last Zulfikár Khán was ordered peremptorily to take the fort. He first allowed Rám Rája to escape, and then pressing the siege, soon became master of the fort. Rám Rája arrived at Vishálgad at the end of

A.D. 1697, and soon went to Sátára, which he made the seat of government. Rámchandra Pant, who had so ably managed the government in his absence, was made Pant Ámát, and one of his kárkúns, Sankráji Náráyan Gaudekar, was made Pant Sachiv, and is the ancestor of the present chief. Timoji Hanwanta, the son of Janárdan Pant, was made Pant Pratinidhi; but he did not keep the office long, as in A.D. 1700 Tárábái bestowed it on Parashrám Trimbak.

Marátha Dissensions, A.D. 1697-1700.

Santáji Ghorpade, the Senápati, had for some time been on bad terms with his lieutenant Dhanáji Jádhav; at last an open quarrel broke out, and Rám Rája took the part of Dhanáji. Santáji's troops deserted him, and he was hunted down and at last surprised and killed in the Sátára districts by Nágoji Máne, deshmukh of Mhaswar, who as a reward was taken into the imperial service. The office of Senápati was given to Dhanáji.

In A.D. 1699, Rám Rája made a plundering expedition on a large scale through Gangthari, Báglán, Khándesh, and Berár, and levied *chauth*. Irritated by this the emperor determined again to attempt the reduction of the hill forts. Leaving his cantonment at Brahmapuri he moved on Sátára. Wasantgad fell first and then Sátára was invested. Aurangzíb pitched his camp near the village of Karinja, his son Ázam Sháh was stationed on the west at Sháhpur, Shirzi Khán on the south, and Tarbiat Khán on the east. Though thus surrounded Sátára held out for several months, as provisions were brought in through the connivance of some of the imperial commanders. This was stopped at last; the defences were mined, and the garrison surrendered. Párli was then attacked and fell in June, and the Mughals retreated to Káwaspur on the Mán river to avoid the rains.

Shiváji II. A.D. 1700-1708.

In the meantime Rám Rája died at Ráygad, leaving two sons, the older of whom, Shiváji, was put on the throne with his mother Tárábái as regent. The war went on as before. In the next few years Aurangzíb reduced all the principal forts from Purandhar to Panhála; but the Maráthás plundered in his rear, and the great families, the Mánkaris, began to side more openly with them. In A.D. 1705, after the capture of Ráygad and Torna, Aurangzíb stayed for some time near Junnar; then marched to Bijápur, and thence to besiege Vákinkera, a village held by Pemnáik, a plundering Berad chief. While engaged here his work in the hills was being undone and the forts were being retaken. Panhála and Pávangad were surprised by Rámchandra Pant, and the former became the residence of Tárábái. Parashrám Trimbak, the Pant Pratinidhi, took Vasantgad and Sátára, while Sankráji Náráyan, the Pant Sachiv, recovered Sinhgad, Ráygad, Rohira, and other forts. After Vákinkera was taken Aurangzíb returned hard pressed by the Maráthás, and reached Ahmadnagar in A.D. 1707. Zulfikár Khán retook Sinhgad; but it was almost immediately regained by Sankráji Náráyan, and in February 1707 Aurangzíb died at Ahmadnagar. With him perished all hope of crushing the Marátha power, and thirteen years after his death Marátha independence was formally recognized by the emperor of Delhi.

The Release of Sháhu.

The grand army under the command of Ázam Sháh at once withdrew from the Dakhan, which was left bare of troops, while the

Part I.
POONA SÁTÁRA AND SHOLAPUR, A.D. 1300-1818.

contest between the sons of Aurangzíb was going on. Hoping to keep the Maráthás occupied by internal quarrels, Ázam Sháh, on his march northwards, released Sháhu the son of Sambháji, under condition of allegiance to the imperial crown. Sháhu gained over to his side several chiefs, among whom were Parsoji Bhonsla, Chimáji Dámodar, Haibatráo Nimbálkar, and Nimáji Sindia, and marched south with a large force. Dhanáji Jádhav, who had been recovering the Poona districts, had defeated Lodi Khán the fauzdár of Poona, and retaken Chákan, marched with the Pratinidhi, Parashrám Trimbak, to oppose Sháhu. The armies met at Khed on the Bhíma, but Parashrám Trimbak, finding he was not supported by Dhanáji, whom Sháhu had secretly gained over, fled to Sátára, while Dhanáji openly joined Sháhu.

The Accession of Sháhu, A.D. 1708.

The united armies now marched by Chandan and Vandan on Sátára; the fort was surrendered by the commander, a Musalmán, who imprisoned the Pratinidhi, and Sháhu entered the city and was formally seated on the throne (March 1708). Dhanáji was confirmed as Senápati, and one of his kárkúns, Báláji Vishvanáth Bhat, the founder of the Peshwa dynasty, now came into notice. Gadádhar Pralhád was made Pratinidhi and Bahiro Pant Pingle Peshwa.

Kolhápur, A.D. 1710.

The war between the two branches of the house of Shiváji went on generally in favour of Sháhu. In the year after his accession Sháhu took Panhála and Vishálgad, but was repulsed in an attack on Rangna. At the end of the year Dhanáji died, and his son Chandrasen was made Senápati in his place. In A.D. 1710 Panhála was retaken by Tárábái, and this fort and the neighbouring city of Kolhápur became her residence and the capital of the younger branch of the family of Shiváji. Tárábái's chief adherents were Rámchandra Pant the Ámát, and Sankráji Náráyan the Pant Sachiv; and in A.D. 1711 Sháhu determined to reduce the territory of the latter chief, which lay round the sources of the Níra. Rájgad had been taken, when the war was ended by the suicide of the Sachiv, and Sháhu took the opportunity to conciliate his party by confirming Náro Shankar the son of the Pant Sachiv in his father's estate and title.

Marátha Quarrels.

Though Sháhu was now firmly seated on the throne, the country was in a state of great confusion; the petty chiefs fortified themselves in their villages and plundered everywhere; and it was some time before order could be restored. The relations between Chandrasen Jádhav and his father's kárkún, Báláji Vishvanáth, had long been far from cordial, and in the year 1713 an open quarrel burst out. Báláji was forced to fly, and first went to Purandhar, where he was refused admittance, and then to Pándugad, at which place he got shelter and where he was besieged by Chandrasen. Sháhu took Báláji's side and ordered Haibatráo Nimbálkar, the sar-lashkar, to raise the siege. He met Chandrasen at Deur, and routed him, whereon the latter retired, first to Kolhapur and then to Nizám-ul-Mulk, the Mughal governor of the Dakhan, who gave him a jáhgir at Bálki. He was accompanied by Ghátge Shirzi Ráo of Kágal and Rambháji Nimbálkar, who afterwards distinguished himself in the Mughal service and received the title of Ráo Rambha, which remained in the family for many years. The office of Senápati was given to Mánáji Moré.

Soon after the arrival of the fugitive chiefs, Nizám-ul-Mulk declared war with Sháhu, who sent Báláji Vishvanáth with a force to join Haibatráo Nimbálkar. A battle was fought near Purandhar with no decisive result, but the Maráthás fell back to the Sálpi pass, and Rambháji Nimbálkar overran the Poona district. After a time Nizám-ul-Mulk withdrew to Aurangábád.

Sháhu's Attempts at Order.

Sháhu now attempted to bring the country into order. A Bráhman named Krishnaráo Khatáokar had collected a body of men in the Máhádev hills, and was levying contributions on all sides. Damáji Thorát had fortified the village of Hingni, forty miles east of Poona, and committed similar depredations. Udáji Chawhán seized the fort of Battis Shirála in the Várna valley, and Sháhu was obliged to win him over by granting him the *chauth* of Shirála and Karád. Báláji Vishvanáth set out to reduce Damáji Thorát, but was treacherously seized by him, and released only on the payment of a large ransom. After his release he marched against Krishnaráo Khatáokar, and with the help of Shripat Ráo, the Pratinidhi's son, routed him at Aundh. Krishnarao then submitted and was granted the village of Khatáo in inám. After this Báláji, who had effected a satisfactory arrangement with Angria, Shiváji's admiral in the Konkan, was in A.D. 1714 made Peshwa in the place of Bahiro Pant Pingle, and he chose Ábáji Pant Purandhare as his Mutálik or deputy, and Rámáji Pant Bhánu, the ancestor of the famous Nána Phadnavis, as his Phadnavis or secretary. Soon afterwards Haibatráo Nimbálkar died, and his office was given to Dáwalshi Somvanshi, whereon his son went over to Nizám-ul-Mulk and received Bársi as a jáhgir. In the meantime Damáji Thorát had seized the young Pant Sachiv, and an expedition was again planned against him. Báláji managed first to effect the Sachiv's release, and in return received the Sachiv's rights in the Poona district and the fort of Purandhar, and Damáji was soon after defeated and taken prisoner.

Rise of the Peshwás, A.D. 1715.

The following year (A.D. 1715) Báláji induced the Mughal officers in charge of Poona to make it over to him, and he began to bring it into order and lay the foundation of the future power of his family. He had become the leading minister of Sháhu, and by his advice the Maráthás began to interfere in the quarrels at Delhi and to attempt to get a formal grant of the territory occupied by them. In A.D. 1718 Báláji marched to Delhi with a force of Maráthás as an ally of the Saiad ministers, and stayed there till A.D. 1720, when he obtained the desired grants of the *chauth* and *sardeshmukhi* of the Dakhan and the sovereignty of the districts south of the Bhíma and north of the Varda and Tungbhadra from Poona to Kolhápur, some parganás in the Karnátak, and several in the Konkan. The districts of Akalkot and Nevása, granted to Sháhu on his marriage by Aurangzíb, were also given up.

Báji Ráo Peshwa, A.D. 1721.

Soon after his return from Delhi Báláji died; and in A.D. 1721 his son Báji Ráo was made Peshwa in his place, though his appointment was opposed by Shripatráo, the son of Parashrám Trimbak, now Pratinidhi. Khanderáo Dábháde, who had been made Senápati in A.D. 1716, also died about this time, and was succeeded by his son

Part I.

POONA SÁTÁRA AND SHOLÁPUR, A.D. 1300-1818.

Trimbakráo, with Piláji Gáikwár as second in command. Báji Ráo while preserving his superiority at home, directed his attention chiefly to conquests in Hindustán, and it was under him that Malhárji Holkar, a Dhangar from the village of Hol on the Nira, and Ránoji Sindia, a Marátha of Kanarkhed near Sátára, rose to note. Another of his officers, Udáji Pavár Vishwás Ráo, now established himself at Dhár in Málwa.

Revival of Family Quarrels, A.D. 1727.

The quarrel between the two branches of the Marátha royal family, which had been slumbering for some time, was revived about A.D. 1727 by Nizám-ul-Mulk, now master of the Dakhan. War followed between the Nizám and Sháhu, in which the former was worsted, and came to terms; but in 1729, Sambháji, rája of Kolhápur, being joined by Udáji Chawhán, crossed the Várna; he was soon surprised by the Pratinidhi and driven back, and Tárábái, the widow of Rám Rája, was taken prisoner and brought to Sátára. The disaster induced Sambháji to make peace, and in A.D. 1730 a treaty was framed by which the Várna and the Krishna were made the boundaries of the two states. Tásgaon, Miraj, and other districts were ceded to Sháhu.

The Dakhan now enjoyed peace for some years, while the Maráthás were engaged in the Konkan Gujarát and Hindustán. Soon after the peace with Kolhápur, Trimbakráo Dábháde, incited by Nizám-ul-Mulk, marched against Báji Ráo to depose him from his superiority; but Báji Ráo, ever on the alert, met him near Baroda and completely defeated him. Trimbakráo fell in the action, and his infant son Yashvantráo was made Senápati, and Piláji Gáikwár was appointed his guardian (A.D. 1731). Ráygad, which since its capture by Aurangzíb had been held by the Sidi of Janjira, was recovered in A.D. 1735. In A.D. 1740 Báji Ráo, the greatest of the Peshwás, died near the Narbada, in the midst of schemes for the conquest of the Dakhan. He had raised himself to a complete pre-eminence among the Marátha chiefs, and had acquired large territories in Málwa, but outwardly he was still subordinate to Sháhu.

Báláji Ráo Peshwa, A.D. 1740-1761.

Báláji was appointed Peshwa in his father's place, though the nomination was opposed by the creditors of Báji Ráo, who had died deeply in debt. A few more years passed quietly in the Dakhan while the Marátha troops overran Hindustán and penetrated into Bengal Orissa and the Karnátak. At last in A.D. 1749, Sháhu, who had long been imbecile, died, and the change which had been impending took place; the sovereignty passed from the Marátha rájás to the Bráhman Peshwás. Sháhu left no direct heirs, and before his death disputes had arisen between his wife Sakwárbái Sirké, who declared for Sambháji the Kolhápur rája, and Tárábái who brought forward a boy whom she called her grandson, Rája Rám, son of Shiváji, who she said had been kept in concealment since his birth. Jagjivan the Pratinidhi, brother of Shripatráo, took the side of Sakwárbái, while Báláji supported the claim of Rám. Immediately Sháhu died, Báláji seized the town and fort of Sátára and took the Pratinidhi and Sakwárbái prisoners. The latter he forced to perform the rite of *sati* or widow-sacrifice, and the former he imprisoned in a hill fort.

Transfer of Sovereignty to the Peshwa, A.D. 1749.

Peshwa Sovereignty.

On the strength of a deed given to him by Sháhu, he assumed the management of the Marátha empire, agreeing to acknowledge the independence of the Kolhápur state and to preserve the jáhgirs of the chiefs. He won over to his side Rághoji Bhonsla, whom he confirmed in his possessions in Berár, as also he did Yashvant Ráo Dábháde in Gujarát, and Fatehsing Bhonsla as rája of Akalkot. The districts in Málwa, conquered by Báji Ráo, were divided between Holkar, Sindia, Pavár, and other chiefs. Jagjivan the Pratinidhi was soon released, but much of his jáhgir west of the Krishna, between the Várna and Urmodi rivers, was taken from him.

The change of rulers was generally agreed in. Yamáji Sevdev, the mutálik of the Pratinidhi, raised an insurrection and threw himself into the fort of Sángola near Pandharpur; but this revolt was at once suppressed by Sadáshiv Bháu, cousin of the Peshwa. Finally, before proceeding to take part in the dispute between the sons of Nizám-ul-Mulk, the Peshwa persuaded the Pant Sachiv to give him up the fort of Sinhgad in exchange for those of Tung and Tikona, and he thus gained the fortress which threatened his capital, Poona. He gave up the fort of Sátára to Tárábái, the rája being kept in the city with a large establishment of attendants.

Rám Rája Entrapped, A.D. 1751.

When the Peshwa had gone (A.D. 1751) Tárábái tried to rouse Rám Rája to revolt. Finding this useless, she sent for Damáji Gáikwár, and on his approach invited the rája into the fort and made him prisoner. The Peshwa's officers in Sátára marched to meet Damáji at Arla on the Krishna, then retired to Nimb, where they were defeated, and Damáji joined Tárábái. Several forts were given up to her, but Nána Purandhare again attacked Damáji and forced him into the Jor Khora, a valley near Wái, where he waited hoping for aid from the Pratinidhi at Karád. The Peshwa hearing of the danger, came up with his army and surrounded Damáji; and then, while amusing him with negotiations, suddenly attacked and took him prisoner and sent him to Poona. Tárábái he left in possession of Sátára and of the person of the rája, as another enemy was pressing on him.

War with the Nizám, A.D. 1751.

The Peshwa had sided with Gázi-ud-dín as a claimant to the Nizám's throne against his brother Salábat Jang; and when the latter by the aid of French troops had secured his succession, he determined to punish the Peshwa, and invaded the Poona districts with the French leader Bussy at the head of a disciplined force. Notwithstanding the efforts of the Marátha army under Máhádáji Pant Purandhare, the Mughals advanced, sacked Ránjangaon, and destroyed Talegaon Dhamdhere. They were there fiercely attacked, and almost routed by the Maráthás, but were saved by Bussy and his artillery, and again advanced as far as Koregaon on the Bhíma. Here Salábat Jang heard that the fort of Trimbak near Násik had been taken by the Maráthás, and returned to Ahmadnagar to get his heavy guns for the siege of the fort. Early in 1752 he moved towards Junnar, but he was harassed by the Maráthás, his troops were mutinous, and danger was threatening from the north, whence his brother Gázi-ud-dín was approaching

Part I.
POONA SÁTÁRA AND SHOLÁPUR, A.D. 1300-1818.

with a large army. He therefore came to terms with the Peshwa, and turned to meet his brother. The whole Marátha force also collected near Aurangábád, and though Gázi-ud-dín was poisoned and war averted, Salábat Jang confirmed a cession of territory promised by Gázi-ud-dín to the Maráthás, comprising the greater part of Khándesh and the Gangthari.

Ráni Tárábái Rebels.

During the absence of the Peshwa Tárábái collected a force of Rámoshis and occupied the Wái and Sátára districts. Her troops were soon driven back and she was besieged in the fort, but the siege was not pressed. Next year (A.D. 1754) Damáji Gáikwár was released and returned to Gujarát after coming to an agreement with the Peshwa about the revenues of that country. He was accompanied by Raghunáth Ráo the Peshwa's younger brother, and their united forces soon took Ahmadábád, and firmly established Marátha supremacy in that province.

Acquisition of Ahmadnagar by the Peshwa, A.D. 1759.

The fort of Ahmadnagar, which had till then been held by the Nizám, was in A.D. 1759 acquired by the Peshwa, who bribed the commander Kavi Jang. Consequently in 1760, the Nizám declared war, but he was defeated by Sadáshiv Bháu at Udgir and forced to make a treaty surrendering the forts of Daulatábád Shivner Asirgad and Bijápur, the provinces of Bijápur, and part of Bidar Ahmadnagar and Aurangábád. Thus Shivner, the birthplace of Shiváji, at last fell into the hands of the Maráthás.

Defeat at Pánipat, A.D. 1761.

The Peshwa Báláji had long been interfering in the affairs of Hindustán, and had incurred the enmity of Ahmad Sháh Abdáli the Afghán king, whose forces Raghunáth Ráo the Peshwa's brother, had driven out of the Panjáb. He advanced in 1759 bent on punishing them, and routed two detachments commanded by Sindia and Holkar with great slaughter. It was necessary to send a larger force to meet him, and in A.D. 1760 the grand army of the Maráthás, with the contingents of all the chiefs, led by Sadáshiv Bháu, marched into Hindustán. After some skirmishing the two armies met at Pánipat in January 1761 and the Maráthás were utterly routed. Sadáshiv Bháu, Vishvás Ráo the Peshwa's eldest son, many other chiefs, and nearly the whole army fell in the fight. Soon after hearing the news Báláji Ráo the Peshwa died (June 1761). The defeat had a decisive effect on the fortunes of the Marátha empire. Up to this time the great chiefs had been generally obedient to the Peshwa, and had always joined his standard. Now his prestige was gone, and the chiefs became more and more independent. Doubtless this might in any case have occurred later; the distant conquests could not long have been controlled from Poona, but the defeat of Pánipat hastened the catastrophe. The minority of Báláji's successor, Mádhav Ráo a boy of sixteen, and the quarrels between him and his uncle Raghunáth, tended to the same result. When Mádhav Ráo grew up, his personal character held together the confederacy for some time; but his early death, and the quarrels as to the succession, decided the matter, and without doubt facilitated the conquest by the English.

Mádhav Ráo Peshwa, A.D. 1761-1772.

Nizám Ali, hoping to profit by the Marátha disasters, declared war, and, though vigorously opposed, advanced to within fourteen miles of Poona, when he was induced to return by the cession of the districts of Aurangábád and Bidar, lately acquired by the Maráthás. Soon afterwards the death of Tárábái (December 1761) relieved the Peshwa's government of an inveterate enemy; the fort of Sátára was surrendered, and Rám Rája, who had been kept a close prisoner there, was allowed to live in the city.

Raghunáth Ráo's Disagreement with the Peshwa.

At first the management of affairs was entirely in the hands of Raghunáth Ráo; but Mádhav Ráo, the young Peshwa, soon became desirous of having a share in the administration, and disputes arose between him and his uncle. The latter retired, and having obtained help from the governor of Aurangábád and collected a large force of Maráthás, marched on Poona, defeated his nephew's army, and again took charge of the government. He made Sakhárám Bápu, a descendant of Gopináth, the Bráhman who betrayed Afzul Khán to Shiváji, and Nilkanth Purandhare, his chief ministers; gave over the fort of Purandhar to the latter, and made several other changes in the ministry. He also, as the price of the aid he had just received, agreed to give back to the Nizám the rest of the provinces ceded in A.D. 1760, but his promise was not kept. The Nizám in consequence declared war, and being joined by Jánoji Bhonsla and other disaffected chiefs marched on Poona in A.D. 1763. As it was an open city, the people fled, and the Mughals sacked and burned Poona; thence they marched to Purandhar, and ravaged the country as far north as the Bhíma. The Marátha army had meanwhile assembled and plundered the Nizám's country; and now, following the Mughals on their return, assailed them as they were crossing the Godávari at Rákshasbhuvan, and inflicted a severe defeat on them, which brought the war to a close. Jánoji Bhonsla, who had deserted the Mughals, was the chief gainer.

Soon after this Mádhav Ráo recovered the management of the government, and kept on good terms with his uncle till A.D. 1768, when Raghunáth retired from court, raised a force and encamped near Dhodap in the Chándod range; but he was soon defeated and taken prisoner, and was kept in custody till the close of Mádhav's reign.

During the four remaining years of his life Mádhav Ráo was chiefly occupied with wars with Jánoji Bhonsla of Berár and invasions of the Karnátak. In one of these wars in A.D. 1769 Jánoji penetrated to Poona and ravaged the country round till peace was made. Mádhav Ráo died in A.D. 1772. His reign may be looked on as the time during which the administration of the country reached its highest excellence; the mámlatdárs and other officers were carefully looked after, the assessment was paid without much difficulty owing to the wealth brought into the country by war, and justice was well administered by the famous Rám Shástri. Mádhav Ráo's chief ministers were Sakhárám Bápu, Moroba Phadnavis, and Moroba's cousin Nána. After Mádhav's death the Marátha empire was plunged in confusion and a period of civil war followed; the great chiefs became completely independent, and an opportunity was given to the English Government to interfere.

Part I.

Poona Sátára and Sholápur, A.D. 1300-1818.

Náráyan Ráo Peshwa, A.D. 1772-1773.

Náráyan Ráo succeeded his brother Mádhav Ráo. Raghunáth, who had been released before Mádhav's death, kept on good terms with Náráyan for a time; but after a few months he interfered in the administration, and was again placed in confinement. In August 1773 a disturbance arose among some of the troops at Poona, and their leaders burst into the palace; Náráyan Ráo took refuge with his uncle Raghunáth, but was followed and murdered in his presence, and there was reason to believe that Raghunáth was implicated in the murder.

Raghunáth Ráo Peshwa, A.D. 1773.

Raghunáth at once assumed charge of the government, but Sakhárám Bápu, Nána Phadnavis, Trimbak Ráo Máma, Hari Pant Phadke, and the other ministers were ill-disposed towards him, and none of his own followers were competent to take their places. Soon after his accession, while he was engaged in war with the Nizám, the old ministers withdrew from his camp to Poona, and having discovered that the widow of Náráyan Ráo was pregnant, had her conveyed in January 1774 to Purandhar, and formed themselves into a regency. Hearing of this, Raghunáth, who had marched into the Karnátak, returned with his army, and was met near Pandharpur by the army of the ministers under Trimbak Ráo Máma. He completely defeated them with the loss of their leader, but instead of marching on Poona, he retired to Burhánpur, and the birth of a son to Náráyan Ráo's widow (April 1774), to whom the name of Mádhav was given, put an end to Raghunáth's chance of success.

The Ministers form a Regency.

Birth of Mádhav Ráo II. A.D. 1774.

First War with the English, A.D. 1775.

Raghunáth retired to Gujarát, hoping to bring there to a successful termination the negotiations for aid which he had already begun with the Government of Bombay. In this he obtained his wish; but the interference of the English was at first limited to Gujarát and the Konkan, and they were soon ordered to suspend hostilities by the Supreme Government of Bengal. Colonel Upton was sent as a commissioner to arrange a peace at Poona, and in March 1776 he signed the treaty of Purandhar, by which the English agreed to give up the cause of Raghunáth.

Treaty of Purandhar, A.D. 1776.

In A.D. 1777, Rám Rája, who for nearly thirty years had been the titular rája of Sátára, died, and was succeeded by his adopted son Sháhu.

A rivalry which for some time had been growing between two of the leading ministers at Poona, Nána Phadnavis and his cousin Moroba, now passed into an open quarrel. Sakhárám Bápu remained neutral, but Moroba was supported by the greater number of the ministers and by Tukáji Holkar. Hari Pant Phadke took the side of Nána, and so did Máhádji Sindia, and though Moroba was at first in the ascendant and Nána had to retire to Purandhar, the position was soon changed when Hari Pant and Sindia came up with their forces and Tukáji Holkar was induced to leave Moroba's party. In July Moroba and his adherents were seized and confined in various forts, and Nána had only one rival left, Sakhárám Bápu.

Second War with the English, A.D. 1778.

The Bombay Government, whose aid had been sought by Moroba, now declared war with the Peshwa's ministry. Their first effort was disastrous. In November 1778 a force occupied the Bor Ghát

Second War with the English, A.D. 1778-1782.

and encamped at Khandála. The main body under Colonel Egerton followed in December, and marched slowly to Kárli, eight miles over level ground in eleven days, constantly engaged with the Maráthás, whose main army was assembled at Talegáon Dábháde under Sindia, Holkar, and Hari Pant, and retired slowly when the English reached that village. Here Colonel Cockburn, who was now in command, embarrassed by his commissariat train, determined to retire, and having thrown his guns into a pond, began his retreat. The Maráthás pressed closely on him, and his rear guard was perpetually engaged till the village of Vadgaon was reached. Colonel Cockburn, despairing of effecting his retreat, began to negotiate, and at last a convention was made through Sindia, by which the English army was allowed to retire on condition of the surrender of the conquests made since the year 1773. This disgraceful convention was at once disavowed by the Bombay Government, and the war was continued. For some months nothing was done, as the Bombay Government awaited the arrival of the army under General Goddard, which was on its march across India. It arrived at Surat in March, and negotiations were carried on till the end of the year. In the meantime Nána Phadnavis, with the connivance of Máhádaji Sindia, got rid of his last rival Sakhárám Bápu, who was thrown into prison and sent to Pratápgad. Before the close of A.D. 1779 negotiations were broken off, and the war was carried on successfully in Gujarát and the Konkan by General Goddard and Colonel Hartley. In the beginning of 1781, General Goddard determined to advance towards Poona, and a detachment forced the Bor Ghát; but when they reached Khandála they were at once attacked in front by the Marátha main army under Hari Pant Phadke and Holkar, while Parashrám Pant Patvardhan was sent with a strong force into the Konkan to assail the flank of the army and cut off its communications with Bombay. After a month of constant fighting, General Goddard was forced to retreat to Bombay with severe loss. The war now languished, and in the beginning of 1782 negotiations were begun with the Poona government through Sindia, and ended in the treaty of Sálbái, by which the conquests in the Konkan were given up with the exception of Sálsette, and a provision was made for Raghunáth Ráo.

Convention of Vadgaon, A.D. 1778.

Treaty of Sálbái, A.D. 1782.

Rise and Death of Sindia, A.D. 1789-1794.

For some years there was peace in the Dakhan, and Sindia was fully occupied in Hindustán warring with the Rájput princes, whom after a hard struggle he worsted. At last in A.D. 1789 he gained possession of Delhi and the person of the emperor, and thus reached the height of his ambition. In A.D. 1790, war broke out between Tipu Sultán of Mysor and the English, and the Maráthás joined as allies of the English and took part in the campaigns of 1790 and 1791, after which Tipu was compelled to sue for peace and surrender a large extent of territory. Soon after peace had been made with Tipu, Sindia marched to Poona, ostensibly to invest the young Peshwa with the insignia of the office of Vakil-i-Mutálik which he had obtained for him from the emperor, but really to supplant Nána Phadnavis and win over the Peshwa. Contrary to Nána's wishes, the Peshwa

Part I.

POONA SÁTÁRA AND SHOLÁPUR, A.D. 1300-1818.

was decorated by Sindia, and a war of intrigue ensued between the rivals, which was only ended by the death of Máhádáji Sindia in February 1794. As Mahádáji's successor was his grand nephew Daulat Ráo, a boy of fourteen, Nána Phadnavis was freed from his most dangerous rival.

The Battle of Kharda, A.D. 1794.

Tedious negotiations had been going on for long between the Nizám and the Peshwa; the Maráthás claimed long outstanding balances of *chauth* and the Nizám made counter-claims. At last, in the end of 1794, war was declared; all the great Marátha chiefs joined the national standard, while the Nizám advanced with all his forces. The armies met near Kharda in Ahmadnagar. In the battle which took place the Mughal army was routed, mainly owing to the cowardice of Nizám Áli, who allowed himself to be shut up in Kharda fort, where he was forced to sign a treaty giving up territory on his western frontier from Purenda to the Tápti.

Death of Mádhav Ráo II. A.D. 1795.

The sons of Raghunáth Ráo, Báji Ráo and Chimnáji, were kept in close confinement by Nána Phadnavis; but the young Peshwa, who was also in complete subjection, opened a correspondence with Báji Ráo. When Nána discovered the correspondence he stopped it at once, and Mádhav Ráo, apparently in a fit of despair, committed suicide on the 23rd of October 1795 by throwing himself from his palace in Poona.

The greatest confusion ensued. Nána Phadnavis, knowing that Báji Ráo, the heir to the throne must be his enemy, summoned the Marátha chiefs to Poona, and persuaded them to agree to the adoption of a son by the widow of Mádhav Ráo. Báji Ráo, though imprisoned in the fort of Shivner, opened communications with Báloba Tátya, one of Sindia's chief advisers, and won him over. Nána, hearing of this, was greatly alarmed, and determined to forestall Báloba, and himself to seat Báji Ráo on the throne. He summoned Parashrám Bháu Patvardhan from Tásgaon, and sent him to Shivner to make the proposal to Báji Ráo, who consented, and came to Poona. Sindia, enraged at his treachery, marched on Poona; Nána Phadnavis, afraid to risk a battle, retired to Purandhar, and thence to Sátára, while Parashrám Bháu and Báji Ráo awaited the arrival of Sindia. By the advice of Báloba Tátya Sindia determined to put Chimnáji, Báji Ráo's younger brother, on the throne; to this Parashrám Bháu agreed, and Chimnáji was installed against his own will in May 1796. Nána Phadnavis had meanwhile retired into the Konkan, where he began to plot afresh for the restoration of Báji Ráo. He won over Sakharám Ghátge Shirzi Ráo, who had joined Sindia's army, and through him Sindia who in October 1796 arrested Báloba Tátya and declared for Báji Ráo. Parashrám Bháu fled, but was captured and thrown into prison. Nána returned to Poona and was reconciled to Báji Ráo, and in December 1796 Báji Ráo was at length formally installed Peshwa. Ahmadnagar and its districts were made over to Sindia as the reward of his help, and Nána Phadnavis again became chief minister. His tenure of power was short. After a year of constant disturbance at Poona, at Báji Ráo's request he was treacherously arrested by order of Sindia

Accession of Báji Ráo, A.D. 1796.

Accession of Báji Ráo, A.D. 1796.

and sent a prisoner to Ahmadnagar. His friends and relations were seized and plundered, and great excesses were committed by Sindia's troops, urged on by Shirzi Ráo Ghátge. Báji Ráo having got rid of Nána Phadnavis, was now anxious to send Sindia away; but as he was unable to pay Sindia the arrears due to his troops, he allowed him to levy the money he wanted from the inhabitants of Poona; Shirzi Ráo Ghátge was employed on this congenial occupation, and executed his orders in the most brutal manner, ill-treating all who were supposed to have money.

Meanwhile trouble was threatening from Sátára. The rája had been allowed, previous to Nána's arrest by Báji Ráo, to seize the fort. He now refused to surrender it, and having collected some troops, drove back a force commanded by Máhádev Ráo Rástia. Parashrám Bháu, who was still a prisoner, offered, if released, to march against the rája. His offer being accepted, he surprised the rája at Sátára, completely routed his troops, and took him prisoner. The rája's brother, Chitúr Singh, escaped to Kolhápur, and with the help of that prince carried on a predatory warfare with considerable success.

The War of The Báis, A.D. 1798 - 1800.

Quarrels which broke out in Sindia's family between him and the Báis or widows of his uncle Mahádaji, reduced him to great difficulties and kept him for some time in the Dakhan. The Báis, who had been grossly ill-treated by Shirzi Ráo Ghátge, were being sent as prisoners to Ahmadnagar, when they were released by a party of Sindia's own horse, and took refuge in the camp of Amrutráo, the Peshwa's adoptive brother. A large party in Sindia's army, disgusted with the tyranny of Ghátge, took part with the Báis. An attempt to surprise Amrut Ráo's camp failed; but when he marched to Poona, Ghátge attacked him suddenly and pillaged his camp at Kirki. At last Sindia was forced to arrest Shirzi Ráo to put an end to his excesses; and in order to obtain money to enable him to return to Hindustán, where his presence was much needed, he determined to release Nána Phadnavis on payment of a large ransom, hoping too that his release would annoy Báji Ráo. In this however he was disappointed, as Báji Ráo soon persuaded Nána to resume his old place as minister (October 1798). Sindia was still unable, through want of money, to leave Poona; the Báis had taken refuge at Kolhápur, and being joined by large numbers of followers, marched northwards, plundering all Sindia's villages, and he was unable to check them. At last by releasing his old minister Báloba Tátya, Sindia was enabled to bring his affairs into some order. An arrangement had been nearly effected with the Báis, when they took alarm and again began plundering. It was not till the year 1800 that, with the help of Yashvant Ráo Holkar, they were driven into Burhánpur and thence to Málwa.

War with Kolhápur, A.D. 1799 - 1800.

The war with Kolhápur and Chitúr Singh had been going on with varying success, till in September 1799 Parashrám Bháu was defeated and killed by the Kolhápur troops. Reinforcements were sent up, and Kolhápur was besieged and would have fallen had not the death of Nána Phadnavis in March 1800 brought about a change of policy.

Part I.
POONA SÁTÁRA AND SHOLÁPUR, A.D. 1300-1818.

Nána's relations and friends were seized and imprisoned, Sindia was allowed to send troops to overrun the jáhgir of the Patvardhan family, and peace was made with Kolhápur.

Sindia and Holkar, A.D. 1801.

At last, in 1801 Sindia marched north to check in person the progress of Yashvant Ráo Holkar. The country he left was in the greatest disorder, ravaged by bands of marauders, among whom was Vithoji, the brother of Yashvant Ráo Holkar, who was taken and executed by order of the Peshwa. Báji Ráo also disgusted the more respectable of his chiefs by his treatment of the Rástia family, the head of which, Mahádev Ráo, was treacherously seized and imprisoned in Ráygad. Yashvant Ráo Holkar, who had at first been successful against some of Sindia's detachments, was completely defeated by him at Indor in October 1801; but he soon rallied his forces and marched south, sending on a detachment under Fateh Sing Máne to ravage Khándesh and the Dakhan. His orders were carried out; the Peshwa's officers were defeated and Khándesh and the Gangthari desolated. Fateh Sing Máne advanced south, defeated a force under Báláji Kunjar at Gár Dhond, and stormed the camp at Bárámati. Sindia sent a large force to the aid of the Peshwa, which, passing Holkar's army, joined the Poona troops, and the united forces took up a position at the Alla pass. Holkar, however, marched south by Ahmadnagar, and thence to Jejuri, joined Fateh Sing Máne, and came down the hills towards Poona, encamping between Loni and Hadapsar. Here he was met by the allied forces, and a battle ensued on the 23rd October 1802, in which he was completely victorious. Báji Ráo fled to Sinhgad, thence to Ráygad, and finally to Máhád in the Konkan; and not feeling safe even there, he took ship and landed at Bassein. Holkar was thus left complete master of Poona. At first he did not abuse his victory. He invited Amrut Ráo to come from Junnar and take charge of the government, which he did after some delay, and allowed his son Vináyak Ráo to be placed on the throne. This being done, Holkar began to plunder the helpless inhabitants of Poona mercilessly, till he and Amrut Ráo were drawn from the city early in 1803 by the approach of the British troops.

Holkar Defeats Báji Ráo, A.D. 1802.

Treaty of Bassein, A.D. 1802.

Báji Ráo, as a last resource, had entered into an alliance with the English, and signed a treaty at Bassein in December 1802, binding himself to keep up a subsidiary army, and not to engage in hostilities without the consent of the English Government. At the same time, with his usual duplicity, he intrigued with Sindia and Raghuji Bhonsla, with the double aim of persuading them to attack Holkar and to make war on the English. The British Government took immediate steps to replace Báji Ráo on the throne. A force under General Wellesley marched from Mysor to Poona, while a part of the Haidarábád contingent moved to Purenda. General Wellesley was joined on his way by the jáhgirdárs of the Southern Marátha Country, and drove before him the plundering bands of Holkar's horse. As it was feared that Amrut Ráo who was hanging about Poona, might burn the city, General Wellesley made a march of sixty miles in thirty-two hours, and arrived there on the 20th April, while Colonel Stevenson moved with the Haidarábád troops to Gárdaund (the present Dhond)

War with Sindia and Holkar, A.D. 1803-1805.

on the Bhíma, and thence to the Godávari. Amrut Ráo retired before General Wellesley to Sangamner, and thence to Násik, which town he sacked. He subsequently came to terms with the English, served with them during the war, and was afterwards pensioned. Báji Ráo was brought back to Poona in May 1803, and General Wellesley took up a position near Ahmadnagar to await the result of the negotiations which were going on with Sindia and Raghuji Bhonsla. These chiefs viewed the treaty of Bassein with much dissatisfaction, and at last war broke out in August 1803; by the close of the year the confederates had been completely defeated at Assaye and Argaon, and peace was made. Next year Holkar forced on a war with the English Government, which lasted for more than twelve months, and was chiefly confined to Hindustán. He too was forced to sue for peace in 1805.

Misgovernment by Báji Ráo.

When Báji Ráo was restored, the country was in the utmost confusion; but with the aid of the British troops the forts were recovered and order partly established. Still his misgovernment and the bad counsels of his chief advisers, Sadáshiv Bháu Mánkeshvar and later on Trimbakji Dengle, prevented the country prospering. Báji Ráo turned off without scruple all the old servants of Government and disbanded the troops. In A.D. 1803 the rains failed, and a fearful famine ensued, aggravated by the war, and the country was nearly depopulated. Great numbers of the disbanded soldiers died and the rest settled in their villages. The Bhils took advantage of the confusion, and plundered the open country, even to the south of the Gangthari; and it was not till years had passed and great cruelties had been exercised, that the Peshwa's officers cleared the country of robbers south of the Chándod range.

Predatory Warfare, A.D. 1805.

In 1805, after the close of the war with Holkar, Fateh Sing Máne, one of his officers, re-appeared in the Dakhan, and began plundering the country south of the Níra till he was attacked and killed by Balvant Ráo Phadnavis, the Mutálik of the Pratinidhi.

Báji Ráo, when he felt secure through the aid of the British troops, endeavoured systematically to depress his jáhgirdárs and centralize his power. He took advantage of quarrels between the Pratinidhi Parashrám Shrinivás and his Mutálik, to interfere on behalf of the latter, and he confined the Pratinidhi at Mhasvad (A.D. 1806). The chief was soon rescued by his mistress, a Telin by caste, and having collected a body of men, began plundering the Sátára district, till he was defeated and taken prisoner by Bápu Gokhle near Vasantgad. His mistress retired to the fort of Vásota in the Ghâts, and held out for eight months (A.D. 1807). The jáhgir was then given over to Bápu Gokhle who levied heavy contributions before he gave it to the Peshwa in A.D. 1811.

Báji Ráo's Crafty Policy.

Báji Ráo next turned on the powerful Patvardhan family, the members of which had never been well disposed towards him, and had neglected to send their contingent of troops. A war, in which other jáhgirdárs would have joined them, was prevented only by the

Part I.
Poona Sátára and Sholápur, A.D. 1300-1818.

interposition of the English Resident, who collected an army at Pandharpur ready to march on them; but the British Government, while enforcing the military service due from the jáhgirdárs, determined to protect them in the possession of the lands lawfully held by them. At a later period Mádhav Ráo Rástia failed to send his contingent, and was stripped of all his lands; and for similar conduct Appa Desái Nipánikar lost a large portion of his jáhgir. In both these cases Báji Ráo had craftily led the jáhgirdárs to disobey orders that he might have an excuse for seizing their lands.

Trimbakji Dengle, A.D. 1813-1814.

In A.D. 1813 Báji Ráo determined to raise a body of disciplined troops commanded by English officers. A brigade was formed and stationed near Poona, as was also a brigade of the subsidiary force, the rest of it being sent to Sirur on the Ghod river about forty miles east of Poona. It was about this time that Trimbakji Dengle reached the height of his power, and under his influence Báji Ráo's government rapidly deteriorated. His one object was to accumulate money; districts were farmed to the highest bidder; no mercy was shown to the farmers who defaulted, and the farmers showed none in their turn to the husbandmen, and made money by the open sale of justice. Trimbakji, who disliked the English, also induced his master to increase his forces, and to intrigue with all the Marátha chiefs. Negotiations had long been going on between the Peshwa and the Gáikwár respecting tribute due to the former, and in 1814 Gangádhar Shástri was sent on behalf of the Gáikwár to Poona. Many efforts were made by the Peshwa to win him over but without success, and at last he was treacherously murdered at Pandharpur by Trimbakji's orders, with the consent of the Peshwa (July 1815). The British Government at once demanded Trimbakji's surrender, and after some delay he was given up and imprisoned in the fort of Thána. In less than a year he managed to escape, and, though in constant communication with the Peshwa, evaded capture by the English by wandering in the hilly parts of the country from Khándesh to Sátára, stirring the wild tribes to revolt.

Rising against the Peshwa, A.D. 1815.

Meanwhile a rising against the Peshwa's authority was spreading in the Ghâts. Chitúr Singh, the brother of the late rája of Sátára, had been seized in Khándesh in 1812 by Trimbakji Dengle and imprisoned in the fort of Kánguri; but in 1816 a Gosávi, with the help of some Rámoshi chiefs, gave out that he was Chitúr Singh, and seized Prachitgad, a strong fort in the hills south of Sátára; several other forts fell into their hands, and the insurrection was never quite quelled by Báji Ráo.

The Surrender of Trimbakji, A.D. 1817.

Trimbakji, assisted by the Peshwa, had since his escape been levying men, and in 1817 a large body assembled at Náteputa, south of the Níra; when the subsidiary force moved against them they retired to Jath, and then turned back to the Máhádev hills north of Sátára, where they were attacked and dispersed. A similar rising took place in Khándesh. At last the Resident insisted on the surrender of Trimbakji, and on a new treaty giving up the forts of Sinhgad Purandhar and Ráygad. Báji Ráo yielded with great reluctance.

A new treaty was signed in May 1817, by which he consented to cede territory for the maintenance of the subsidiary force and the fort of Ahmadnagar, to recognize the settlement with the jáhgirdárs in 1812, and to restore Mádhav Ráo Rástia's jáhgir. The three forts were given back in August, as the Peshwa appeared to be complying with the treaty. In reality he was making preparations for the war which soon broke out.

War with the Peshwa.

The Governor General had for some time been concerting measures for suppressing the Pendháris and restoring order in Central India. Accordingly by the end of the rains the greater part of the British troops were sent north to take part in the operations. The Peshwa, seeing his opportunity, proceeded rapidly with his preparations for war, promising all the time to send his troops north to aid the British forces. At last, as the Resident suspected his sincerity, the small force at Poona was moved to a position at Kirki, and was reinforced by a European regiment from Bombay, and on the afternoon of the 5th of November A.D. 1817 the long-determined attack was made by the Peshwa's troops; 26,000 Maráthás assailed a British force numbering 2800 men, and were decisively repulsed. General Smith who commanded the subsidiary force, had already begun his march from the Gangthari on Poona, and on his approach the Peshwa returned to Máhuli near Sátára, and there brought the rája of Sátára into his camp. The English commander, after occupying Poona, followed Báji Ráo, who returned hastily to Pandharpur, and then up the Bhima, past Junnar, and on to Bráhmanváda, where he occupied a strong position in the hills; but General Smith, marching round by Ahmadnagar and Sangamner, headed him, and he again fled south. On the news of his approach a detachment of the subsidiary force had been summoned from Sirur to Poona, and on the 1st of January 1818 reached Koregaon on the banks of the Bhima, and found the Marátha army of 25,000 men on the opposite bank. Though only 800 strong, the detachment held the village all day long against the assaults of the Marátha army, and at night the enemy retired baffled and continued their flight south. After a long and futile chase, it was determined to reduce Sátára, and the fort surrendered on the 10th of February 1818. A detachment was then sent to take the other hill forts, and the rest of the army under General Smith resumed the pursuit of Báji Ráo, who had been staying near Sholápur. He was overtaken on the 20th of February at Ashti, and in the skirmish Bápu Gokhle his general was killed and the rája of Sátára taken. Thence Báji Ráo fled to Kopargaon on the Godávari and waited for help from Holkar; but being disappointed, again started, and after long wanderings surrendered to Sir John Malcolm at Dholkot in May 1819.

Battle of Kirki, A.D. 1817.

Battle of Koregaon, A.D. 1818.

Báji Ráo Surrenders, A.D. 1819.

Peshwa's Territories.

Meantime the English troops had taken the Peshwa's country. Chákan was captured by a force under Colonel Deacon; Sinhgad Purandhar and Vásota, where two European officers were confined, fell after short sieges by April 1818, and Pratápsinh was formally installed rája of Sátára on the 14th of April 1818. A force under

Part I.
POONA SÁTÁRA AND SHOLÁPUR, A.D. 1300-1318.

Peshwa's Territories Conquered, A.D. 1818.

General Munro had marched north from the Karnátak, occupying the forts on the way; they routed a body of Báji Ráo's infantry under the walls of Sholápur, and stormed the fort on April 13th, 1818. Ráygad, where the Peshwa's wife had taken refuge, was surrendered on the 7th of May, and during the same month the forts to the north of Poona were reduced by Major Eldridge. The last fort to fall in this part of the country was Prachitgad, held by the false Chitursingh, which was captured on the 13th of June. Thus the territory of the Peshwa was completely conquered by the English. Out of this territory it was thought politic to assign a part as a principality for the titular rája. A tract extending from the Níra to the Várna and from the Gháts to the Bhíma was reserved for him, but was for the time placed under the management of a British officer, Captain Grant Duff, until the young rája could gain experience. The other districts were put in charge of officers whose powers resembled those of the sarsubhedárs, and the superintendence of the whole country was entrusted to a Commissioner, Mr. Elphinstone.

Conspiracy against the English.

For a time troops were stationed at the chief places, Karád, Sátára, Sholápur, Poona, Sirúr, and Junnar, and many of Báji Ráo's levies accepted service. They were however disbanded as soon as possible, and the hill forts were dismantled. At first no one was allowed to travel armed without a passport; but this restriction was soon relaxed and the country remained quiet. Soon after the conquest a conspiracy for the expulsion of the English was discovered at Poona and Sátára, but the prompt execution of the ringleaders, among whom were some Bráhmans, had a good effect in preventing the recurrence of such attempts.

Treaty with Landholders, A.D. 1818.

Treaties were entered into with the jahgirdárs, and they were dealt with in accordance with their standing and their behaviour to the British Government during the war. The land of the old Mánkaris, such as the Nimbálkars of Phaltan, the Daphles of Jath, and the Ghorpades of Mudhol, were restored to them intact, as were those of the great officers of the Marátha rájás, the Pant Sachiv, the Pratinidhi, and the rája of Akalkot. All these chiefs, with the exception of the Ghorpades, were placed at their own wish under the rája of Sátára; the lands of the Patvardhan family, which had risen under the Peshwás, were restored to them, as they had taken the English side at an early opportunity, and even chiefs like the Rástiás and the Vinchurkar, who had followed Báji Ráo to the last, were allowed to retain their personal estates.

Sátára Annexed, A.D. 1848.

In April 1822 the Sátára territory was formally handed to the rája, and thenceforward was managed by him entirely. After a time he became impatient of the control exercised by the British Government, and as he persisted in intriguing and holding communications with other princes in contravention of his treaty, he was deposed in A.D. 1839 and sent as a state prisoner to Benares and his brother Sháhji was put on the throne. This prince, who did much for the improvement of his territory, died in A.D. 1848 without male heirs, and after long deliberation it was decided that the state should be resumed by the British Government. Liberal pensions were granted to the rája's three widows, and they were allowed to live in the palace at Sátára. The survivor of these ladies died in 1874.

Since A.D. 1848 no events of political importance have taken place in these districts. Throughout the Mutinies of 1857 peace was maintained and no open outbreak took place, though the mutiny of a regiment at Kolhápur gave rise to uneasiness, and there was undoubtedly a good deal of disaffection at Sátára among the classes whom the resumption of the country had impoverished. In Poona too the doings of Nána Sáheb, the adopted son of the last of the Peshwás, could not fail to create an excitement among the Bráhmans, who felt that power had passed out of their hands, and who would gladly have regained it.

Leading Marátha Families: *Under the Bhonslás.*

Of the Marátha families whose names figure constantly in history, the first are the Mánkaris or honourables, the old families who held lands previous to the rise of the Bhonsla dynasty. Mention has already been made of the Sirké family, the old rulers of the Ghát Mátha, who were dispossessed by the Morés. They have always held high rank among the Maráthás, and were frequently connected by marriage with the rájás of Sátára. The conquest of the Ghát country by Shiváji from the Morés, the rájás of Jávli, has also been mentioned. Members of the family were conspicuous as soldiers, and one of them was for a time Senápati. The Nimbálkars of Phaltan, whose surname was originally Pavár, are one of the oldest Marátha families. They have been deshmukhs of Phaltan since time immemorial, and were confirmed in their rights by the kings of Bijápur. Though connected by marriage with the Bhonslás, they continued faithful to Bijápur till the fall of the monarchy. In the reign of Sháhu, one of the family was sar-lashkar, and another member sided with the Mughals and obtained the jághir of Karmála and the title of Ráo Rambha. The Phaltan jáhgirdár is one of the chiefs with whom the British Government has entered into a treaty. He was placed under the rája of Sátára and bound to furnish a fixed number of horse, and since the resumption of the state he has been placed under the Collector of Sátára. His jáhgir is a strip of country lying between the Níra river on the north and the Mahádev hills on the south; it is about 400 square miles in extent and yields a gross yearly revenue of about Rs. 1,00,000. Frequent failure of the rainfall prevents the district from being a fertile one, but it is fairly prosperous. Other branches of the Pavár family distinguished themselves under Sháhu and the Peshwás, and founded the states of Dhár and Dewás in Central India. The Daphles of Jath, whose original name was Chawhán, take their present name from the village of Daphlápur, of which they were pátils. They held a *mansab* under the Bijápur kings, but never rose to any great eminence afterwards. A separate treaty was made with them as with the chief of Phaltan. Jath lies to the south-east of the Sátára district, not far from Bijápur, and is neither fertile nor populous. Its area is about 700 square miles and its gross yearly revenue about Rs. 1,70,000.

Part I.

POONA SÁTÁRA AND SHOLÁPUR, A.D. 1300-1818.

Leading Marátha Families: *Under the Bhonslás.*

The Mánes of Mhasvad were from an early period deshmukhs of part of the Mán desh, and were powerful chiefs. They sided with the Bijápur government against Shiváji; and one of them, Nágoji Máne, made himself notorious by the murder of the gallant Santáji Ghorpade, an action for which he was rewarded by a place in the imperial service. The family never attained to any distinction under the Peshwás. The Ghátges of Khatáv were deshmukhs of Málavdi in the Mán desh, and held a *mansab* under the Bahamani kings. They also received a sanad as sardeshmukhs from Ibráhim Ádil Sháh in A.D. 1626. Another house of the same name, with the title of Shirzi Ráo, came from Kágal near Kolhápur. One of this family is infamous as the evil-adviser of Daulut Ráo Sindia, and the instigator and executor of the sack of Poona in 1797. The Ghorpades of Kápsi near the Várna and of Mudhol near the Ghatprabha furnish several well-known names. The original surname of the family was Bhonslé, and the tradition is that the present name was won by an ancestor who scaled a steep Konkan fort by the help of a string tied to the tail of an iguana or *ghorpad*. The most celebrated of this family was Santáji, who was Senápati from A.D. 1691 to 1698, and during that time was the terror of Mughal detachments. He fell a victim to the jealousy of his colleagues, and his sons left the Marátha service and established themselves at Sondur and Guti in the Karnátak. Murár Ráo (the Morary Row of Orme) was a member of this family, and was a conspicuous character in the war between the English and French on the Coromandel coast. He was reconciled to the Maráthás under Mádhav Ráo, but never kept up a close connection with them. His fate was a sad one. Guti, his capital, was taken by Haidar Ali, and he was thrown into prison, where he died. Of this family too was Báji Ghorpade, the chief who seized Shiváji's father Sháhji, and who was afterwards surprised and killed by Shiváji.

Under the House of Shiváji.

Next we come to the families who owe their rise to Shiváji and his house. The story of the rájás of Akalkot is romantic. When Sháhu was marching southwards on Sátára after his release in the year A.D. 1707, his troops had a skirmish with some villagers, and in the middle of the fight a woman came and laid her child at Shahu's feet. He took it up and adopted it, giving it in place of its own surname Lokhande, the name of Fateh Sing Bhonsla. Though not a man of any great ability, the adopted son of Sháhu took part in the wars of the time, and received the jáhgir of Akalkot in the Sholápur collectorate. The Akalkot chief was one of those with whom the British Government entered into a treaty; and he was put under the rája of Sátára and is now under the supervision of the Collector of Sholápur. The area of the state is about 500 miles and the gross yearly revenue about Rs. 3,25,000.

Of the ministers of the Sátára rájás two only retain any position. The Pratinidhi, whose office was not one of the eight created by Shiváji, but was made by Rája Rám in A.D. 1680 for Pralhád Niráji, his chief adviser, who accompanied him to Jinji. The office was supposed to entitle the holder to take precedence of the Asht Pradháns. The first of the present family who attained distinction was Parashrám,

Leading Marátha Families: *Under the House of Shiváji.*

Trimbak. He brought himself into notice as a subordinate of Rámchandra Pant, the officer in charge of the Sátára territory during Rám Rája's absence at Jinji, and was made Pratinidhi in A.D. 1700 by Tárábiá; having opposed Sháhu on his return, he was deprived of his office in 1708, but restored in A.D. 1720. His son Shripat Ráo, who was Pratinidhi from A.D. 1720 to 1747, was the able opponent of the Peshwás, and his brother and successor Jagjivan attempted to prevent the transfer of power to them in A.D. 1749; he was, however, no match for his crafty rival, and was imprisoned, and lost a considerable portion of his jáhgir near Sátára. The family continued to hold a large part of the eastern districts of Sátára, which they had originally recovered from the Mughals, till the rebellion of the young chief, already mentioned, in A.D. 1806. He was restored to the portion of his estates that remained in A.D. 1818, when a treaty was made with him, and he was placed under the rája of Sátára. The Pratinidhi is now like the other jáhgirdárs under the charge of the Collector of Sátára. His possessions consist of the Atpádi Mahál in the Mán desh, and a number of detached villages. His gross yearly income is about Rs. 2,00,000. The Pant Sachiv was one of the Asht Pradháns, and the office became hereditary like most of the others instituted by Shiváji. The founder of the present line was Sankráji Náráyan Gaudekar, who was appointed to the post in A.D. 1698 by Rám Rája. He distinguished himself by recovering the country round the source of the Níra from the Mughals, and it has been ever since held as the jáhgir of his family. He also had in his possession Sinhgad and Purandhar. He was among the chiefs who opposed Sháhu, but when he committed suicide in A.D. 1712, his son Náru was confirmed in the post. Purandhar was given by the Pant Sachiv to Báláji Vishvanáth Peshwa in A.D. 1714 in return for his services in releasing the young chief from Damáji Thorát; and Sinhgad was exchanged for Tung and Tikona in A.D. 1750. A treaty was entered into with this chief in A.D. 1818, similar to that made with the other jáhgirdárs; and he too is now under the Collector of Sátára. His estate of Bhor is an extensive but hilly tract lying along the Gháts to the west of Poona; its area is about 1500 square miles, and its gross yearly revenue is about Rs. 3,75,000, a good deal of which is derived from the chief's assignment on the revenue of certain districts called the Sahotra Amal. The Dabháde family rose into importance under Sháhu, and in 1716 Khanderáo Dábháde was made Senápati. The chief scene of his exploits was Gujarát, where he gained a firm footing. His son Trimbakráo was one of the opponents to the rise of the Peshwás, but he was defeated and killed at the battle of Dabhoi in A.D. 1731 by Báji Ráo. Though his child Yashvantráo was made Senápati in his place, the family never recovered their former position, but were supplanted by their subordinates, the Gáikwárs, the present rulers of Baroda. The representative of the Dábhádes now holds only the two villages of Talegaon and Induri, some twenty miles north-west of Poona.

Under the Peshwás.

Of the families who rose to greatness under the Peshwás, the most important was that of the Patvardhans, but their history does not

Part I.

POONA SÁTÁRA AND SHOLÁPUR, A.D. 1300-1818.

Leading Marátha Families.

Under the Peshwás.

come within the scope of this summary. When Báláji Vishvanáth was serving as a kárkún under Dhanáji Jádhav the Senápati, one of his fellow-kárkúns was A'báji Purandhare, kulkarni of Sásvad, a village eighteen miles south-east of Poona. When Báláji was made Peshwa in 1714, A'báji Purandhare became his mutálik or deputy, and the family were ever after faithful servants of the Peshwás, and acquired great influence. They still hold a high position among Bráhmans. The Rástiás rose to great power under the earlier Peshwás; but Báji Ráo took a strong dislike to the family, which was represented in his reign by Mádhav Ráo and Khande Ráo. In A.D. 1801 he treacherously imprisoned the former, and in A.D. 1815 deprived him of his jáhgir; still the family served him throughout his last war with the English, and thereby forfeited considerable possessions. The Vinchurkar family, who were equally faithful to Báji Ráo, have been mentioned in another section (Part II. page 633), as the larger portion of their estates lies in the Gangthari.

DAKHAN HISTORY:

MUSALMÁN AND MARÁTHA,

A.D. 1300 - 1818.

Part II.—Khándesh Násik and Ahmadnagar.

BY

W. W. LOCH Esquire,

BOMBAY CIVIL SERVICE.

[Contributed in 187[illegible].]

DAKHAN HISTORY.

PART II.

Part II.

KHÁNDESH NÁSIK AND AHMADNAGAR. A.D. 1300-1818.

Early History.

LITTLE is known of the territories included in Ahmadnagar Násik and Khándesh previous to the Musalmán invasions at the close of the thirteenth century. The ancient remains, the rock temples of Ajanta, Ellora, of Pátna in the Sátmála hills, of Násik and Junnar with their elaborate carvings and paintings, and the fine old wells and temples which are found throughout these districts and known by the name of Hemádpanti, show that at different periods before the arrival of the Musalmáns the inhabitants had risen to a considerable height of civilization and prosperity. The author of the Periplus (A.D. 247) mentions that Dachanabades that is the Dakhan, from its two cities, Tagara whose site is doubtful and Plithana the modern Paithan on the Godávari, carried on trade with Barygaza or Broach. In Khándesh traditions of the shepherd kings or Gauli rájás, to whom are attributed some old remains, such as a tank hewn out of the solid rock in the Songir fort and the walls of the Turan Mal fort, probably chiefly belong to the Devgiri Yádavs. The old dam to the lake of Turan Mal is attributed to the god Goraknáth. Hiuen Thsang, the Chinese Buddhist pilgrim who visited Maháráshtra early in the seventh century of the Christian era, talks of its great capital near a great river, probably Násik on the Godávari, and its warlike inhabitants governed by a Kshatriya king.

The Devgad Kings.

The capital of the Dakhan was afterwards moved to Devgad or Daulatábád; and there, at the time of the first Musalmán invasion in A.D. 1294, reigned a king of the Yádav family. His power probably extended over the open country of Daulatábád Ahmadnagar and Násik. The hilly country of Bágián and of Gálna about fourteen miles north of Málegaon was held by independent rájás, while the Sátpuda hills near Nímár belonged to a race of Ahírs or shepherds, the last of whom, Ása the Shepherd King, is said to have built the fort of Asírgad shortly before A.D. 1370.

Musalmán Invasion. A.D. 1294.

In A.D. 1294 Ala ud-dín Khilji, during the reign of his uncle Jelál-ud-dín, emperor of Delhi, invaded the Dakhan through Berar with 7000 horse, surprised Rámdev Yádav the king of Devgad, and extorted from him a large tribute, before the rájás of Khándesh and Gulbarga, whom he had summoned, could come to his aid. Ala-ud-dín then retired to Hindustán through Khándesh.

Conquest of the Dakhan, A.D. 1312.

In A.D. 1306 Malik Kafur, Ala-ud-dín's general, invaded the Dakhan through Sultánpur, a province of Khándesh, and overran Maháráshtra. Rámdev remained tributary to the Musalmáns till his death. His son revolted but was defeated, and Devgad his capital was taken in A.D. 1312. Maháráshtra then became part of the Delhi empire: a governor was

Part II.

KHÁNDESH NÁSIK AND AHMADNAGAR, A.D. 1300-1818.

placed at Devgad, and Berar and Khándesh were formed into a separate province. In A.D. 1316 a second insurrection headed by Hirpal Dev, a cousin of the last chief, was successful for a time, but was put down in A.D. 1318.

The Bahamani Dynasty, A.D. 1347-1500.

In A.D. 1344 the Musalmán nobles of the Dakhan revolted against Muhammad Tughlak, and by A.D. 1347 they established their independence. They chose for their king the general who had taken the leading part in the war; and his dynasty is known as the Bahamani dynasty. It lasted for about 150 years. The capital at first was at Gulbarga and then at Bidar. The territory included the districts of Násik and Ahmadnagar; but the rájás of Báglán and Gálna maintained their independence; and Khándesh remained for some time longer under the Delhi sovereigns. Farishtah speaks of a rája of Antur, and more than a hundred years later the forts of Antur and Vairagad were in the hands of the Maráthás, from which it would appear that the Bahamani kings had not a firm hold of the country about the Sátmála hills. A governor was stationed at Daulatábád, and ruled a province comprising Cheul in the Konkan, Junnar, Daulatábád, and Mhiropatan or Maháráshtra.

For many years the western districts enjoyed peace. A rising took place at Daulatábád in A.D. 1366 headed by one Bahrám Khán, aided by a Yádav chief and by the rája of Báglán; the rebels marched to Paithan, and the king's troops encamped at Shevgaon. In the engagement that followed the rebels were routed, mainly through the impetuous attack of king Muhammad Sháh.

The Kingdom of Khandesh, A.D. 1370.

About A.D. 1370 the districts of Thálner and Kurunda in Khándesh were given by Firúz Tughlák of Delhi to Malik Rája an Arab adventurer. He attacked the rája of Báglán and forced him to pay tribute; and also invaded Sultánpur, which belonged to Gujarát, but was driven back into Thálner. He died in Thálner in A.D. 1399, and he and several of his successors were buried there. Thálner was given to his younger son, and the rest of his possessions to Malik Názír his elder son, who is considered the first king of Khándesh and the founder of the Faruki dynasty. Malik Názír married the daughter of Muzaffar Sháh of Gujarát, and though there was not unfrequently war between them, the Khándesh princes usually acknowledged the supremacy of the kings of Gujarát.

Soon after his accession Malik Názír seized by treachery the fort of Asirgad from A'sa the Ahír; and at the advice it is said of Shaikh Zeinudín, a sage of Daulatábád, he built the towns of Burhánpur and Zeinábád on the Tápti. Burhánpur became the capital of Khándesh and one of the most important towns south of the Narbada, standing on one of the highways between Hindustán and the Dakhan. In A.D. 1417, with the help of the king of Málwa, Málik Názír recovered the fort of Thálner from his brother; took Sultánpur and overran Nandurbár in A.D. 1420, but his troops were soon driven out by the Gujarát army. In A.D. 1435 he invaded Berar, which was then subject to the Bahamani kings, but he was attacked by Ala-ud-dín Bahamani, who took Burhánpur and ravaged Khándesh. Málik Názír took refuge in the fort of Laling, but was defeated and besieged by

The Kingdom of Khándesh, A.D. 1370.

the Dakhan troops in A.D. 1437. He died during the siege, which was raised on the approach of aid from Gujarát. The Khándesh dominions appear to have included the country between the Sátpudás and the Tápti as far west as Thálner, which was a frontier fort, and as far east as Burhánpur and Ásirgad; and to the south of the Tápti, the country from Zeinábád up to the Sátmála hills, as far west as Laling, which was also a frontier fort.

Malik Názir was succeeded by his son Miran Ádil Khán. He was assassinated in A.D. 1441, and his son Mubárik Khán reigned till A.D. 1457. Ádil Khán then became king, and his reign, which lasted till A.D. 1503, was one of the most flourishing periods of Khándesh history. He neglected to pay tribute to Gujarát, but was forced to do so about the year 1499.

Independence of Ahmadnagar, A.D. 1489.

Towards the end of the fifteenth century the Bahamani dominions had become greatly extended, and they were redistributed into eight provinces, of one of which Daulatábád was the head, and of another Junnar. About A.D. 1485 these provinces were placed under Malik Ahmad Beheri, who made Junnar his head-quarters, and employed himself in reducing the petty Marátha chiefs. His father, Nizám-ul-Mulk, was murdered at Bidar in A.D. 1489, and Malik Ahmad threw off his allegiance to the Bahamani kings. He defeated the first force sent against him; and when a second army was sent he retired to Junnar, and then marched to Jeur, a village near the source of the Sína river. The Bahamani troops marched by Tisgaon to Bhingár, and remained inactive there for nearly a month, till Malik Ahmad suddenly marched across from Jeur, surprised and routed them. This victory secured the independence of the kingdom of Ahmadnagar and the power of the Nizám Sháh dynasty as the line of Ahmad is called; and about the same time Yusúf Ádil Sháh made himself independent at Bijápur. The history of the Dakhan for the next century and a half is the story of a succession of wars between the Muhammadan kings of Khándesh, Berar, Ahmadnagar, Bidar, Golkonda, and Bijápur; and till the completion of the Mughal conquest of Ahmadnagar in A.D. 1637, hardly a year passed in peace, and the state of the country, especially round Sholápur, must have been miserable. Khándesh was more fortunate than the Dakhan, and till the Maráthás began their depredations it enjoyed comparative rest. Under its own kings and under the Mughals it was one of the richest countries in India. Under the Mughals Burhánpur was the head-quarters of a royal viceroy, and the aqueducts and the remains of the palaces and mosques attest its former importance. The population of the country was large, irrigation was common, and districts such as Navápur Sultánpur and the Pál Tappa, now almost deserted on account of their unhealthy climate, were formerly thickly peopled and highly cultivated.

When Malik Ahmad had ensured his own safety, he endeavoured to secure the fort of Daulatábád. His first efforts were unsuccessful, and he then determined to build his capital in a central situation near the scene of his victory at Bhingár. In two years (A.D. 1493-1495) a city sprang up, which, says Farishtah, equalled in splendour Bagdad and Cairo and was called by its founder's name. There are now at

Ahmadnagar no buildings which can compare with those of its rival, Bijápur; a few tombs and the aqueducts and fort are almost the only memorials of the Musalmán rulers; but while Bijápur is deserted by trade Ahmadnagar is still one of the most thriving towns in the Dakhan. Ahmad built a palace and made a garden where the present fort stands, and brought water in three aqueducts from Kapurvádi, a distance of about five miles. On the capture of Daulatábád he built a mud fort which about the year A.D. 1560 was replaced by the present stone building. Ahmad is said to have built the palace of which the ruins remain at the Bhisti Bág. He and his successors were buried in the Roza Bág, close to the city, where their tombs still stand.

In A.D. 1499 Mahmúd Begada, sovereign of Gujarát, overran Khándesh; and Ahmad Nizám Sháh marched to Burhánpur to help A'dil Khán Faruki of Khándesh: their united forces drove Mahmúd back, but next year he returned and exacted tribute from A'dil Khán. When Ahmad returned from Khándesh, he again attacked Daulatábád, and at last took it. About this time the kings of the Dakhan mutually acknowledged each other and settled the boundaries of their respective kingdoms. That of Ahmadnagar comprised the present districts of Daulatábád, Ahmadnagar, the open country of Poona and Násik, and part of the Konkan. Ahmad Nizám Sháh is said to have reduced the fort of Antur and other places in the Sátmálás, and to have made the rájás of Báglán and Gálna pay him tribute. On the death of A'dil Khán of Khándesh in A.D. 1503, his brother Dáud Khán came to the throne, and reigned till A.D. 1510. His death was the signal for confusion till A'dil Khán II. was put on the throne by his grandfather Mahmúd of Gujarát.

Ahmad Nizám Sháh died in A.D. 1508, and was succeeded by his son Burhán, during whose long reign (1508-1553) Ahmadnagar was constantly at war with Bijápur. The cause of quarre. was the right to Sholápur and the adjoining five districts. These had been promised to Burhán by Ismáel A'dil Sháh as the dowry of his sister, who was married to Burhán in A.D. 1523. The districts were not given at the time; Burhán overran them in A.D. 1543, and gave them back, and finally in 1549 with the aid of the kings of Bidar and Bijánagar he took Sholápur. In A.D. 1526 Burhán took from the king of Berar the district of Pathri the home of his ancestors, overran Berar, and routed the Khándesh forces; but in A.D. 1528 Bahádur Sháh of Gujarát came to aid them, drove back the Ahmadnagar troops, and occupied Ahmadnagar, while Burhán retired to Junnar. Bahádur Sháh built the black terrace (where the present *kacheri* stands), and remained in the city forty days, when he was compelled to retire for want of provisions, and was followed by Burhán to Daulatábád, where peace was made. In that year and in A.D. 1530, when Burhán met him at Burhánpur, Bahádur Sháh's supremacy was acknowledged.

A'dil Khán II. of Khándesh died in A.D. 1520. He was succeeded by Miran Muhammad, who took part as an ally of Bahádur Sháh in the war just mentioned. When Bahádur Sháh died in A.D. 1535, his heir Mahmúd was a prisoner at Asirgad in the hands of Miran Muhammad, who took advantage of this and had himself proclaimed king of Gujarát. He died in six weeks, and his brother Mubárak, who succeeded him on the throne of Khándesh, released Mahmúd but obtained from him the provinces of Sultánpur and Nandurbár as his ransom. These provinces remained from that time part of the Khándesh kingdom, and an attempt made in A.D. 1566 by Chengiz Khán, a Gujarát general, to retake them, was defeated, after he had penetrated as far as Thálner. Mubárak reigned till 1566. He was the first of the Khándesh kings who came in contact with the Mughals. In A.D. 1561 Báz Bahádur was expelled from Málwa by Akbar; the Mughal forces followed him into Khándesh and sacked Burhánpur, but were overtaken and routed by Mubárak.

In A.D. 1553 Hussain Nizám Sháh succeeded his father Burhán and soon became involved in war with A'li A'dil Sháh, who was aided by Rámráj of Vijayanagar, while the king of Golkonda sometimes sided with one party sometimes with the other. The allies advanced and besieged Ahmadnagar, but were forced to retire for want of supplies. Hussain then built the present stone fort, and carried the war into the districts near Sholápur; but having suffered a severe defeat near Kalyán, in which he is said to have lost 600 cannon, among them the great gun now at Bijápur, he had to retreat to Junnar, while the allies once more besieged Ahmadnagar (A.D. 1562). The rains came on, and a flood of the Sina is said to have carried away 25,000 men of Rámráj's army. The allies retreated, and the Musalmán kings, alarmed at the insolence of Rámráj, combined against him. Hussain gave his sister Chánd Bibi to A'li A'dil Sháh in A.D. 1563, with Sholápur as her dowry, and the united forces invaded the Vijayanagar territories. A decisive battle was fought at Tálikot on the Krishna in which Rámráj was killed and his army routed. Soon after this Hussain died and was succeeded by his son Mortiza, a madman. He overran Berar, defeated the Khándesh troops who opposed him, and by A.D. 1572 annexed it to the kingdom of Ahmadnagar. As he grew older he secluded himself entirely, and entrusted the management of the kingdom to Salábat Khán, a minister who has left a high reputation for ability and integrity. He is said to have begun the tank at Bhátodi near Ahmadnagar, which has lately (1877) been restored; and his tomb on the hills to the east of the city is a prominent feature in the landscape. He was dismissed and imprisoned about the year A.D. 1585, because the king considered that he was responsible for a war with Bijápur; he was released in A.D. 1588 after Mortiza's death, and died in A.D. 1589. Mortiza was killed in A.D. 1587 by his son Mirán, who reigned only a short time being assassinated by his minister Mirza Khán, and Ismáel was put on the throne in 1588. Akbar, the emperor of Delhi, seized the opportunity for interference in the affairs of the Dakhan, and favoured the claims of Burhán the brother of Mortiza. Ibráhím A'dil Sháh also took Burhán's side. He was at first unsuccessful, but in A.D. 1590 he defeated Ismáel's troops and became king.

In Khándesh Mubárak, who died in A.D. 1566, was succeeded by his son Mirán Muhammad. It was this prince who interfered unsuccessfully on behalf of Berar in 1571. He died in 1576 and was succeeded by his brother Rája Ali.

Part II.

KHÁNDESH NÁSIK AND AHMADNAGAR, A.D. 1300-1818.

The Nizám Sháh Dynasty, A.D. 1489-1600.

In A.D. 1594, Burhán Nizám Sháh died and was succeeded by Ibráhím, who was killed the same year in battle with Bijápur. The nobles of Ahmadnagar were divided into four factions, and the chief who held the city, and had in his power the infant king Bahádur Sháh, called in the Mughals. Their army drew near the city under the command of Murád, son of Akbar, but the approach of danger made the nobles unite to defend their capital. Chánd Bibi, the widow of A'li A'dil Sháh and aunt of the young king, threw herself into the fort; persuaded the king of Bijápur to march to her aid; and by her gallant defence forced the Mughals to raise the siege and retire (A.D. 1595). A temporary peace followed and Berar was surrendered to the Mughals.

Next year (A.D. 1596) fresh disturbances broke out at Ahmadnagar, and Murád again marched into the Dakhan with Rája A'li of Khándesh as his dependant and ally. The kings of Golkonda and Bijápur joined the Ahmadnagar forces, and a great battle was fought in January 1597 at Sonpat on the Godávari with no decisive results. Rája A'li was killed in the fight, and was succeeded by his son Bahádur Khán.

Akbar Conquers Khándesh, A.D. 1599.

Akbar now marched in person to carry on the war, and arrived at Burhánpur in the year A.D. 1599. Disagreements arose between him and the king of Khándesh, and Akbar overran Khándesh and blockaded Asirgad, where the king took refuge. Meanwhile Akbar's son, prince Dániál, had advanced on Ahmadnagar; the place was in utter confusion; the soldiers murdered Chánd Bibi, and a few days later the Mughals stormed the fort and took the king prisoner (July 1600). Shortly afterwards Asirgad surrendered; the king was sent a prisoner to Hindustán, and Khándesh became part of the empire of Delhi. Prince Dániál was made governor of Khándesh and Berar; his capital was at Burhánpur; and for a time Khándesh was called after him Dándis, and copper coins were struck at Burhánpur called Dánpaisa.

Sháh Jahán takes Ahmadnagar, A.D. 1617.

The Nizám Sháh dynasty did not become extinct on the fall of the capital. Malik Ambar, an Abyssinian, set up Mortiza as king, retired across the Godávari, and founded a city at Kharki near Daulatábád, to which Aurangzíb afterwards gave the name of Aurangábád. He defeated the Khán-i-Khánán the Mughal leader, and re-took Ahmadnagar and Berar. In A.D. 1612 he drove back another army and forced it to retire into Báglán, and it was not till A.D. 1617 that he was defeated by Sháh Jahán and forced to surrender Ahmadnagar, which thenceforward remained in the hands of the Mughals. He died in A.D. 1626. Malik Ambar was not more famous for his skill as a general than for his revenue administration; and the settlement made by him was preserved in Sháhji's jáhgir round Poona, though in many districts it was supplanted by Todar Mal's settlement. It was under him that the Marátha chiefs became important. The greatest family was that of the Jádhaves of Sindkhed, whose chief went over to the Mughals in A.D. 1621. The Jádhaves were descendants of the rájás of Devgad; and the villages of Hatnur, Bansendra, and Bokangaon not far from Ellora are still held by the family. The Bhonslás of Verola or Ellora, from whom came Shiváji, were another important family.

In A.D. 1628 war broke out on account of Khán Jahán Lodi, the

Part II.

KHÁNDESH NÁSIK AND AHMADNAGAR, A.D. 1300-1818.

End of the Nizám Sháh and Burhánpur Dynasties, A.D. 1631-1637.

Mughal governor of the Dakhan, who was suspected by Sháh Jahán and took refuge in Báglán. The Deshmukhs refused to surrender him to the Mughals, and drove back their forces, but Khán Jahán was at last obliged to fly, and was afterwards overtaken and killed. In A.D. 1631 Mortiza Nizám Sháh was killed by the son of Malik Ambar, and Daulatabad was taken by the Mughals in A.D. 1633. Sháhji Bhonsla, the father of Shiváji, set up another king, and overran the country south of the Chándod range and as far east as Ahmadnagar; in A.D. 1634 he drove back the Mughals from Purenda and forced them to retire to Burhánpur, but fresh forces were sent, and in A.D. 1637 he came to terms and surrendered the Nizám Sháh prince, and thus the kingdom of Ahmadnagar was extinguished.

Mughal Period.

In A.D. 1633 Khándesh was made into a *subha*, and included part of Berar and the present district of Khándesh as far south and west as Gálna. The districts of Sultánpur and Nandurbár had formerly been joined to the *subha* of Málwa. The country south of Khándesh as far as the Bhima was made into a separate *subha*, of which Daulatabád was the head. Both governments were in 1636 united under Aurangzíb. He reduced the hilly country of Báglán, which was however soon relinquished. In the years of quiet which now succeeded Sháh Jahán introduced into his Dakhan possessions a new revenue system known as that of Todar Mal. This assessment called *tankha* was the standard assessment till the British revenue survey system was introduced. In 1616 Sir Thomas Roe passed through Khándesh and was received at Burhánpur by prince Parvis. The city had not then recovered from the ravages of the late wars, and contained few fine buildings. Forty years later it was visited by the French traveller Bernier, and about A.D. 1665 by Tavernier, who travelled up from Surat. At that time there was a considerable trade in brocades and muslins. Tavernier mentions Nandurbár as famous for its musk melons and grapes and for its careful and hardworking husbandmen. In A.D. 1670 the English factory was moved from Ahmadábád to Nandurbár.

Maráthá Incursions, A.D. 1657-1678.

Before the middle of the seventeenth century Shiváji, the founder of the Marátha empire, had begun to establish himself in the western hills. In A.D. 1657 he ventured to attack the Mughal territory, and surprised the town of Ahmadnagar. He was driven off, but carried away considerable booty. Profiting by the confusion which ensued on the struggle for power between the sons of Sháh Jahán, Shiváji extended his ravages, and scarcely a year passed without incursions into the Ahmadnagar districts. The fort had gained a reputation for strength since its successful defence by Chánd Bibi, and the Maráthás never ventured to attack it. In A.D. 1664 Shiváji sacked the town and retired with his plunder. After his return from Delhi in A.D. 1666, he began hostilities on a more extended scale. In 1670, after sacking Surat, he retired through Khándesh by the pass near Sálher. A few months later he sent Pratáprão Gujar into Khándesh, and he for the first time exacted from the village officers promises to pay *chauth*. At the same time Moro Pant Trimal took the forts of Aundh and Patta in the Akola district and the important fortress of Sálher in Báglán, which commanded one of the great roads into Gujarát. Aundh and Patta were re-taken by the Mughals in the same year, and in A.D. 1672 Mohabat Khán besieged Salher. Shiváji sent a force to raise the siege, which was attacked by the Mughal troops; after a severe action the Mughals were completely routed, the siege was raised, and the lost forts were recovered.

Shivaji's Death, A.D. 1680.

In A.D. 1673 Khán Jahán was sent to the Dakhan, but the usual incursions continued, and finally Khán Jahán cantoned at Pedgaon on the Bhíma, and built a fort which he called Bahádurgad; and from that time Pedgaon became an important frontier post of the Mughals. Shiváji's attention was for some time directed to other quarters, but in A.D. 1679 he crossed the Bhíma and plundered the country up to Gálna; on his return he was attacked near Sangamner on his way to Patta. He drove back the first body which attacked him with considerable difficulty, and was proceeding on his way, when he found the road blocked by another body of troops, and only the superior knowledge of his guides enabled him to avoid the enemy and reach Patta in safety. Shiváji then reduced all the forts round Patta. He died in the following year (1680). In A.D. 1684 the emperor Aurangzíb left Hindustán and reached Burhánpur with the grand army of the empire. He sent on two armies, one under his son Moázim by Ahmadnagar to the Konkan, the other under his son Azim to reduce the Chándod country. Sálher was given up, but the Mughal army was completely repulsed by the *havaldár* of the fort of Rámsej near Násik, and retired. Patta and the other forts were reduced by the Mughals. Aurangzíb advanced to Ahmadnagar in A.D. 1685, and even while he was there the Marátha troops moved up from the Konkan, ravaged the whole of Khándesh, sacked Burhánpur, and returned plundering by Násik. Till A.D. 1707 Aurangzíb was detained in the Dakhan engaged in a weary and fruitless contest with the Maráthás, and in that year he retreated hard pressed to Ahmadnagar, where he died on the 21st February 1707. He was buried at Roza.

Decline of the Delhi Empire, A.D. 1708.

Owing to the dissensions between the sons of Aurangzíb the Mughal power in the Dakhan rapidly declined. In A.D. 1716 Dáud Khán, governor of the Dakhan, revolted against the Saiads, who then ruled at Delhi in the name of the emperor Farukshir; he was, however, defeated and slain in a battle in Khándesh by Hussain A'li Saiad. Hussain A'li then sent troops to open the communication between Burhánpur and Surat, which was stopped by Khanderáo Dábháde, a Marátha leader, but they were surrounded and cut to pieces by that chief. A larger force was then sent, and a battle was fought near Ahmadnagar; the result was indecisive, but the advantage remained with the Maráthás. At last after tedious negotiations, through the able management of Báláji Vishvanáth the Peshwa, the Maráthás obtained in A.D. 1720 the grant of the *chauth* and *sardeshmukhi* of the six divisions of the Dakhan including Ahmadnagar and Khándesh. Shortly after this, the withdrawal of imperial power from the Dakhan was completed by the revolt of Nizám-ul-Mulk, governor of Málwa. He crossed the Narbada in A.D. 1720: Asirgad and Burhánpur were surrendered to him, and

Recognition of Marátha Claims, A.D. 1728.

Part II.

KHÁNDESH NÁSIK AND AHMADNAGAR. A.D. 1300-1818.

the whole of Khándesh acknowledged his authority. He then defeated one imperial army at Burhánpur and another at Bálápur in Berar, and from that time was practically independent. Ahmadnagar and the Gangthari were subject to him as well as Khándesh.

The Nizám, A.D. 1750.

Nizám-ul-Mulk died in A.D. 1748 at Burhánpur, and the Peshwa took advantage of the disturbances which followed his death to attack his successor Salábat Jang. The Peshwa had however miscalculated his power, as Salábat had as his general the Frenchman Bussy. The Nizám advanced to Ahmadnagar in A.D. 1751. Bussy repelled the attacks of the Maráthás and surprised their camp at Rájápur on the Ghod river. As it advanced the Nizám's army plundered Ránjangaon and destroyed Talegaon Dhamdhera. A severe action was fought here, and the Nizám's troops were nearly routed, but they advanced to Koregaon on the Bhíma. News then arrived that the fort of Trimbak near Násik had been surprised by the Maráthás, and Salábat Jang returned to Ahmadnagar; in A.D. 1752 he marched thence by Junnar to retake the fort, but being hard pressed by the Maráthás he agreed to an armistice. He was the more ready, as he was threatened by an attack from his eldest brother Gázi-ud-din, who advanced with a large army to Aurangábád, and promised the Maráthás to cede them the country between the Tápti and the Godávari west of Berar. Gázi-ud-dín was poisoned while at Aurangábád, but his brother Salábat confirmed the cession, and thus the Maráthás gained the greater part of Khándesh Násik and the Gangthari.

Khándesh ceded to the Maráthás, A.D. 1752.

The Peshwa Gains Ahmadnagar, A.D. 1759.

In A.D. 1759 the Maráthás at length gained the fort of Ahmadnagar. It was betrayed to the Peshwa for a sum of money by the Nizám's commandant Kavi Jang, whose descendants still hold some *inám* villages in Karjat to the south of Ahmadnagar. War ensued between the Peshwa and the Nizám; the Maráthás began by taking the fort of Pedgaon on the Bhíma; they then attacked the Nizám at Udgir and forced him to come to terms (A.D. 1760). He surrendered the forts of Daulatábád, Sinnar, Asirgad, and Bijápur; confirmed the surrender of Ahmadnagar, and gave up the greater part of the provinces of Bijápur Bidar and Aurangábád. By this treaty the whole of the present district of Ahmadnagar and part of that of Násik were gained by the Maráthás. Next year they suffered the disastrous defeat of Pánipat, and the Nizám, taking advantage of their distress, advanced, burned the temples of Toka at the meeting of the Pravara with the Godávari, marched on Poona, and forced the Peshwa to restore some of the districts lately ceded.

Cession of Ahmadnagar and Násik, A.D. 1760.

Quarrels among the Maráthás.

In A.D. 1762 quarrels arose between the Peshwa Mádhav Ráo and his uncle Raghunáth; and the latter, in order to gain the help of the Nizám, agreed to restore the remainder of the districts ceded in A.D. 1760. A treaty was made to that effect at Pedgaon, but as the quarrels in the Peshwa's family were adjusted, the treaty was not carried out. Consequently in A.D. 1763 the Nizám marched on Poona and burnt it. As he retired he was overtaken by the Maráthás; and part of his army was attacked by them at Rákshasbhuvan on the Godávari and cut to pieces. After this defeat the Nizám came to terms and confirmed the former cessions.

Part II.

KHÁNDESH, NÁSIK AND AHMADNAGAR, A.D. 1800 - 1818.

Raghunáth Peshwa in Khándesh, A.D. 1774.

In A.D. 1767 fresh quarrels broke out between Mádhav Ráo and his uncle. Raghunáth levied troops in the Gangthari and encamped near the fort of Dhodap in the Chándod range; but his forces were defeated by Mádhav Ráo, and he was taken prisoner. In A.D. 1774, after Raghunáth had defeated the army of the Bráhman ministers at Pandharpur, he marched to Burhánpur and thence to Málwa; and then hoping to gain followers in Gujarát, he moved to Thálner in Khándesh, garrisoned it, and proceeded to Surat. Thálner was soon reduced by the Ministers' troops.

The English now took part in the quarrels among the Maráthás. In 1778 the first English force marched across India under Colonel Goddard, who, after reaching Burhánpur, pursued the route through Khándesh to Surat. The war was finished in A.D. 1782 by the treaty of Sálbái, and Raghunáth retired to Kopargaon on the Godávari in the Ahmadnagar district, where he soon after died. His family remained there till A.D. 1792, when they were removed to Anandveli near Násik.

The Peshwa and the Nizám, A.D. 1795.

In A.D. 1795, in consequence of the Peshwa's exorbitant demands, war broke out between him and the Nizám. The Nizám marched as far as Kharda in the south of the present district of Ahmadnagar and was met there by the Maráthás. The issue of the engagement which ensued was for some time doubtful, till the Nizám took fright and retired into the fort of Kharda, where he was shut up and forced to sign a treaty surrendering districts along the frontier from Purinda to Daulatábád. This was the last occasion on which all the great Marátha chiefs acted together.

Cession of Ahmadnagar to Sindia, A.D. 1797.

With the death of Mádhav Ráo II. in A.D. 1796, a time of confusion and trouble, unparalleled even in Indian history, began, and quiet was not restored until the conquest of the country by the English in A.D. 1818. In A.D. 1797 Sindia, who had already obtained large grants of land in the Ahmadnagar districts, received the fort of Ahmadnagar and other lands in the neighbourhood as the price of his support of the claims of Báji Ráo to be Peshwa. At the end of the same year he seized and imprisoned in the fort the great minister Nána Phadnavis. In A.D. 1798 disputes between Daulatráo Sindia and the two elder widows of his adoptive father Mahádaji Sindia resulted in the war known as the war of the Báis; their troops ravaged the parts of the Dakhan subject to Sindia, and the country round Ahmadnagar suffered severely. Nána Phadnavis was released, and at last in A.D. 1800 Sindia obtained the help of Yashvant Ráo Holkar, who attacked the Báis in Khándesh and drove them into Burhánpur, whence they managed to escape to Mewár.

Holkar Wastes Khándesh, A.D. 1802.

Soon after this war broke out between Holkar and Sindia. From A.D. 1802 when Holkar devastated Sindia's possessions in Khándesh may be reckoned the ruin of this once flourishing province. Holkar marched on plundering through the Gangthari; he routed Narsinh Vinchurkar, who opposed him, and advanced to Poona; then followed the battle of Poona, which left the Peshwa at the mercy of Holkar. As his only resource Báji Ráo signed the treaty of Bassein with the English, and the English forces marched on Poona. Colonel

Part II.

KHÁNDESH NÁSIK AND AHMADNAGAR, A.D. 1300-1818.

Advance of the English on Poona, A.D. 1803.

Stephenson with the Haidarábád army took up a position at Purenda, while Sir A. Wellesley advanced to save Poona from Amrut Ráo the adopted brother of Báji Ráo (April 1803). Amrut Ráo retired to Sangamner, ravaging the country, and then turned off to Násik, sacked it, and remained in that neighbourhood till the end of the war, when he made terms with the English. The common danger made the Marátha chiefs unite against the English. During the negotiations previous to the outbreak of the war Sir A. Wellesley marched to Válki, eight miles south of Ahmadnagar. On the 8th of August he stormed the town, on the 10th his guns opened on the fort, and on the 12th it was surrendered. Wellesley then crossed the Godávari, and on the 23rd of October fought the battle of Assaye. In October Colonel Stephenson took Burhánpur and the fort of Asirgad, and Sindia was forced to make peace. By the treaty of Sirji-Anjangaon, Burhanpur Asirgad and his Khándesh possessions were restored to Sindia, while Ahmadnagar and its districts were given to the Peshwa. The war against Holkar still continued, and his districts in the Dakhan were taken by the English. Chándod, Gálna, and other forts were surrendered and in A.D. 1805 he came to terms. His possessions with the exception of Chándod Ambar and Shevgaon were at once restored, and these districts also were given up within two years.

Ahmadnagar Restored to the Peshwa.

The Famine of 1803.

To add to the miseries of the country, which had been ravaged by several armies, the rains failed in 1803, and a fearful famine ensued. Whole districts were depopulated; the survivors took refuge in the forts built in the larger villages; the Bhíls and other wild tribes took advantage of the confusion, collected in large bands, and completed the ruin of the land; they pillaged and murdered without mercy, and none was shown to them in turn.

Báji Ráo, A.D. 1803-1818.

Under Báji Ráo districts were farmed to the highest bidder; the farmer had not only the right to collect the revenue, but to administer civil and criminal justice; as long as he paid the sum required and bribed the favourites at court, no complaints were heard; justice was openly bought and sold; and the mámlatdár of a district was often a worse enemy to the people than the Bhíls. Under the former Peshwás Khándesh had been treated as a separate province and placed under a sarsubhedár, whose power sometimes extended over Báglán. Báláji Ráo added a second sarsubhedár named Báloba Mandavagani over the country between the Godávari and the Nira, but on his death no successor was appointed. Báji Ráo appointed one Báláji Lakshman as sarsubhedár of Khándesh and Báglán with full powers to put down the Bhil disturbances. At the instigation of Manohirgir Gosávi, who commanded some troops under him, Báláji invited a large body of Bhíls to a meeting at Kopargaon on the Godávári. He there treacherously seized them, and threw them down wells. He cleared the country south of the Chándod range for a time, but in Khándesh the Bhíls became desperate, and plundered more than ever. In A.D. 1806 a second massacre of Bhíls by the Peshwa's troops took place at Ghevri Chandgaon in the Shevgaon táluka of Ahmadnagar. In Khándesh the villages of Chálisgaon and Dharangaon and the fort of Antur were the scenes of other atrocities.

Part II.
Khándesh Násik and Ahmadnagar, A.D. 1300-1818.

When Trimbakji Dengle was in power he was ordered to put down the disturbances which had again risen to a great height. He commissioned Nároba Takti, pátil of Karrambha, to clear the Gangthari and 5000 or 6000 horse and a large body of infantry were given him. The pátil butchered the Bhíls wherever found, and all who had any connection with them without any distinction of caste. During fifteen months it is said that 15,000 human beings were massacred.

The Pendhári Freebooters, A.D. 1816.

In 1816 Trimbakji, who had been imprisoned at Thána in the Konkan for the murder of Gangádhar Shástri, escaped and wandered about the hilly country of Khándesh Báglán Násik and Sangamner, rousing the wild tribes, and making preparations for war in concert with his master. The Pendháris who had not hitherto ravaged Khándesh or the Dakhan also began to make inroads. In A.D. 1817 Godáji Dengle, Trimbakji's brother, rose in Khándesh: his force was dispersed by Lieutenant Davies with some of the Nizám's cavalry, but they re-assembled and took a fort. The British armies were now collecting to crush the Pendháris, and in October 1817 General Smith, who was in command at Sirur, marched to guard the Chándod passes; but early in November, hearing that affairs were threatening at Poona, he concentrated his troops at Puntámba on the Godávari. On the 5th of November Bájiráo's power was overthrown at Kirki. While General Smith marched on Poona, Báji Ráo fled north, past Junnar to Bráhmanváda in the hills south of Akola. General Smith then marched to Ahmadnagar, which had surrendered, and thence over the Nimbdhera pass to Sangamner; the Peshwa hearing of his movements fled south, and was followed by the British army over the Vashira pass and south towards Poona. After a long pursuit the Peshwa was overtaken in February 1818 at Ashti in Sholápur. A skirmish ensued, and in March 1818 he again fled to Kopargaon, his old home on the Godávari. After a time he went on to Chándod, but hearing that a British force was approaching from the north, he returned to Kopargaon, and thence fled east, and finally surrendered in May at Dholkot near Asirgad. In the meantime Holkar and the Pendháris had been defeated, and by the treaty of Mandesar in January 1818, Holkar surrendered to the English all his possessions south of the Sátpudás. Sir T. Hislop marched into Khándesh and summoned the fort of Thálner belonging to Holkar. The commandant at first refused to surrender, but, as the troops were preparing to storm the place, he came out and gave himself up; a few of the troops entered, when some mistake arose, and the Arab garrison cut them down and with them two officers; the fort was at once stormed, the garrison put to the sword, and the commandant hanged. This example told, and the other forts were rapidly surrendered. At the end of A.D. 1817, a Bráhman named Dáji Gopál collected a few followers and drove the mámlatdár out of the fort of Betávad, south of the Tápti; he held the place and levied contributions till he heard of the fall of Thálner, when he evacuated the fort. The strongholds in the Ahmadnagar hills were reduced by Major Eldridge and those in the Chándod range by Lieut.-Colonel McDowall. The Arab mercenaries of the Peshwa collected in the strong fort of Málegaon,

Establishment of Peace, A.D. 1819.

built fifty years before by Náro Shankar Rája Bahádur, to make a last stand, and defended themselves with such obstinacy that the place was not taken till the 13th of June 1818. With the fall of Asirgad on the 9th of April 1819 the war ended. The whole of the Peshwa's dominions and those of Holkar in the Dakhan were taken by the British Government. In Khándesh Sindia held the districts of Ráver, Varangaon, Edlábád, and Páchora, and in Ahmadnagar half of Shevgaon and the Shrigonda pargana. Ráver and Páchora were finally made over to the English Government in 1843-4, and the other districts were taken in exchange in 1860 for territory given to Sindia. The greater part of the Korti district was under Ráo Rambha Nimbálkar till 1821, when it was given over to the English. Khándesh was placed under Captain Briggs, and Ahmadnagar with the country between the Chándod hills and the Bhima under Captain Pottinger. Little difficulty was experienced in restoring order in Ahmadnagar; the country was exhausted and the people willingly obeyed any power that could protect them; the Peshwa's disbanded soldiers settled in their villages; the hill forts were dismantled, and their garrisons gradually reduced. Near the Sahyádris the country was in the hands of the Koli Náiks; they and the Bhíl Náiks were sent for, and the allowances and villages which they already held were confirmed to them on the understanding that they should keep the adjoining country quiet. In a short time the Ahmadnagar districts enjoyed a peace to which they had long been strangers.

In Khándesh the pacification of the country was more difficult. The Bhíls formed a large portion of the population, and though the open country was soon cleared, it was not so easy to reduce the mountainous tracts of the Satpudás and the unhealthy wilds of the west. A considerable force was kept up, which had its head-quarters at Málegaon: the hills were guarded and outbreaks were severely punished. On the other hand inducements were held out to the Bhíls to cultivate land; two agencies were established, one for the western Bhíls and one for those in the eastern and southern districts called the Kanar agency; advances were made and land given free to all who would settle; allowances were made to the Náiks who held the hill passes; and finally attempts were made to give the Bhíls employment by forming them into an irregular force. Owing to the lazy habits of the men and their dislike of discipline, the first efforts failed. It was not till A.D. 1825 that Lieutenant (afterwards Sir James) Outram was successful in forming the Bhíl Corps. His patience and firmness, combined with his thorough knowledge of their character, gave him a great influence over his men; they soon did good service against bands of plunderers, and Khándesh by degrees grew quiet.

The Country at the British Conquest.

When the British Government took possession of the country much of it was almost ruined. Of Khándesh the Honourable Mountstuart Elphinstone, in his report on the territory conquered from the Peshwa, says: Some parts of the province are still in high cultivation, and others, more recently abandoned, convey a strong notion of their former richness and prosperity; but the greater

Part II.

Khándesh Násik and Ahmadnagar, A.D. 1300-1818.

British Management.

part of Khándesh is covered with thick jungles, full of tigers and other wild beasts and scattered with the ruins of villages. The districts north of the Tápti in particular, which were formerly very populous, and yielded a large revenue, are now almost an uninhabited forest. Further on he says: The east of Gangthari, though open and fertile, is almost entirely uninhabited since the famine of 1803; the country between that and Ahmadnagar is better, and the plains south of Ahmadnagar are for many marches in all directions one sheet of the richest cultivation.

As examples of the condition of the country it will be enough to notice that in A.D. 1803 only twenty-one out of 180 villages were inhabited in the Nevása táluka of Ahmadnagar, a district of the Gangthari. In other parts of the same collectorate, in A.D. 1819, more than half the land was waste and all the country round Sirur was unpeopled. In the Chopda táluka of Khándesh, north of the Tápti, only four per cent of the land was cultivated in A.D. 1818. The city of Ahmadnagar contained in 1818 a population of 13,000, and in three years this number was almost doubled. In Khándesh new towns, such as Dhulia Párola and Jalgaon, sprang up. Land was taken for cultivation on easy terms, and when, after some years of experience, the Revenue Survey was introduced, the progress of the country towards prosperity was steady.

Bhíl Rising in 1857.

Since the country came under British management the only notable disturbances are those caused by the outbreak of the Bhils in 1857. The Bhíls were excited by the mutiny in Hindustán, and rose in the Ahmadnagar district in October 1857. A skirmish took place in that month between a body of Bhíls under Bhágoji Náik and the police under Captain Henry, in which Captain Henry was killed. Other risings occurred in Khándesh in the Sátpuda Hills under one Kajar Singh, and in other parts and also in the Nizám's territory in the country to the north and west of Aurangábád. Detachments were sent out, and levies made, and after several skirmishes and some loss of life the greater number of the bands were broken up; but it was not till November 1859 that the disturbances were finally put down by the total destruction of Bhágoji Náik's band by Mr. (the late Sir) Frank Souter, and a force of police, and the dispersal of one or two other bands at the same time in the Nizám's territories. In Khándesh the town and fort of Párola, which belonged to a member of the Jhánsi family, were confiscated by Government and the fort dismantled.

Chiefs and Jahgirdárs.

The number of important chiefs or jahgirdárs connected with these districts is small. In the wild west of Khándesh thirteen petty states are under the charge of the Collector as Political Agent. Of these six are known by the name of Mewas and seven by the name of Dángs; the former are situated north of the Tápti about the Sátpuda hills, and the latter south of the Tápti and below the Gháts. The chiefs are the descendants of the Bhil Náiks who held the western districts when the British power was established: the districts are unhealthy and thinly peopled; the revenue of the chiefs is derived principally from timber dues; they are allowed to settle all petty disputes themselves, and serious cases

Part II.

KHÁNDESH NÁSIK AND AHMADNAGAR, A.D. 1300-1818.

Chiefs and Jáhgirdárs.

go before the Collector. One of the principal states in the Sátpudás was the Akráni pargana held by a Rájput. Its early history is unknown. After the decline of Musalmán power, Chaoji, rána of Dharwai, north of the Narbada, established himself in the hilly part of the country. He was succeeded by his son Gaman Singh, who built the Akráni fort; and he in turn by his son Hanmant Singh; his son and successor Gaman Singh died without heirs, and great disturbances ensued till Bháu Singh, rána of Maltwar, a district on the west, annexed the country and built the fort of Roshmal. He was succeeded by his son Bhikáji, who murdered Jangar, the Bhíl Náik of Chikli, below the hills; and in revenge Jangar's son Deváji surprised Roshmal and killed Bhikáji. On this the Peshwa's troops occupied the country, and when a year later the British forces conquered Khándesh, Akráni submitted to them. The present rána has an *inám* village, Pratáppur, and an annual allowance in lieu of the Akráni pargana. To the south of the Dángs is the small state of Surgána, which belongs to the deshmukh of the district; it is also under the supervision of the Collector of Khándesh. Further south, and also below the Ghâts, the Musalmán state of Peint remained under the care of the Collector of Násik until on the death without heirs of the Begam in 1878 it lapsed and became a subdivision of the district of Násik. The most important jáhgirdár is the Vinchurkar, a Bráhman whose ancestors rose into note under the Peshwás; he holds a number of villages in the Gangthari and lives at the town of Vinchur in the Násik collectorate. The family rose to importance in the middle of the eighteenth century when Vithal Shivdev was at its head; he distinguished himself at the siege of Ahmadábád in 1755, and accompanied the Marátha army in the fatal expedition which ended in the defeat of Pánipat (A.D. 1761), of which he was one of the few survivors. He was raised to high rank by Ragunáth Ráo. The family acquired large possessions in Hindustán, but these were forfeited on account of their adherence to Báji Ráo.

The most noteworthy of the Khándesh jáhgirdárs are the Dikshits of Shendurni, the descendants of Paltankar Dikshit, the priest or *guru* of Báji Ráo, the last Peshwa. The grant of this jáhgir was confirmed by the British Government at the special request of Báji Ráo.